EPIC SURVIVAL

EPIC SURVIVAL

Extreme Adventure, Stone Age Wisdom, and Lessons in Living
from a Modern Hunter-Gatherer

MATT GRAHAM
and JOSH YOUNG

Gallery Books

New York   London   Toronto   Sydney   New Delhi

G

Gallery Books
An Imprint of Simon & Schuster, Inc.
1230 Avenue of the Americas
New York, NY 10020

First Gallery Books hardcover edition July 2015

GALLERY BOOKS and colophon are registered trademarks of Simon & Schuster, Inc.

For information about special discounts for bulk purchases, please contact Simon & Schuster Special Sales at 1-866-506-1949 or business@simonandschuster.com.

The Simon & Schuster Speakers Bureau can bring authors to your live event. For more information or to book an event contact the Simon & Schuster Speakers Bureau at 1-866-248-3049 or visit our website at www.simonspeakers.com.

Interior design by Robert E. Ettlin

Manufactured in the United States of America

1   3   5   7   9   10   8   6   4   2

Library of Congress Cataloging-in-Publication Data is available.

ISBN 978-1-4767-9465-5
ISBN 978-1-4767-9468-6 (ebook)

This book is dedicated to anyone who is willing to view the natural world as a gift and to appreciate, enjoy, preserve, and learn from it.

CONTENTS

CONTENTS

EPIC SURVIVAL

Introduction

HEART OF THE WILD

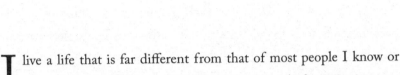

I live a life that is far different from that of most people I know or have read or heard about. Yet it is a life upon which our society was built. While most people's lives are calibrated by ones and zeros, the daily beat of city streets, and the frenetic demands of modern-day living, mine is dictated by the wild. At first glance, mine is far more dangerous.

For the past twenty years, I have all but ignored the digital age and pursued a hunter-gatherer lifestyle, living as man did many thousands and even hundreds of thousands of years ago. This has taught me that the wilderness is a place of truth that will accept and enhance the life of any person who is ready to live on its terms.

Many people who try hard to enjoy life end up feeling empty and cannot figure out why. For me, the solution to happiness has lain on green meadows, rocky passes, and flowing streams. The wilderness needed to be explored and better understood. Once I made that decision, I felt released from the chains of society. My legs would take me to the places I needed to go. If they couldn't carry me there, I didn't need to be there.

I've walked into the wilderness wearing only a loincloth and a pair of handmade sandals and carrying a blanket, a stone knife, and a bag of chia seeds. Once I lived there alone for half a year and tested the limits of what a person can endure physically and mentally. My body went through amazing physical changes. The caked tartar flaked off my teeth and my breath became sweet, and my thinning hair filled back in. I also adapted physically. After my body virtually crashed while eliminating toxins, I bounced back and could run like a wild animal and spear a fish from twenty yards. All my senses were heightened, and I found that the more my body was tested, the more energy I was able to draw from the land to sustain me.

For most of my life, I have lived off the grid in traditional-style wickiups, pit houses, and primitive structures with no electricity or plumbing, remote places all, ranging in location from the mountains of Utah to the bottom of the snow-covered Grand Canyon to the jungle of Kauai in a hut built out of banana leaves. I have made fires out of bark, vines, sagebrush, tamarisk twigs, and a cow's anklebone to stay warm and cook my food. To survive, I became a proficient hunter using the atlatl, a device for throwing a spear that gives it greater velocity, and was accomplished with it to the point that I once beat the world atlatl champion in competition.

I have run thousands of miles exploring every piece of the wilderness in the western United States that called to me. On these treks, I wear handmade sandals constructed from yucca fibers to keep me closer to the earth. I've run through the Sierra Nevada mountains, the Mojave Desert, the Sonoran Desert, the Grand Canyon, Death Valley, and up the middle of California. In these explorations, I interacted with the plants and the animals. I was in no hurry. I didn't want to be just another alien visitor. If I sensed I had something to learn from a particular place, I would stay for days, or even weeks at a time, and listen to what the land had to offer.

But I don't mean to brag in the least, nor do I want to push my lifestyle on anyone. I am interested in sharing my explorations of the land.

I want to show what the human body and mind can do when pushed to its utmost limits, and how nature can help take care of it. I hope to add a dimension to people's lives through what I have experienced and what I have seen.

One of the most important things I've learned from living off the land is that it makes you more observant. Today in our lives—and I know because I have stepped out of the wilderness for periods of time—we can become desensitized to the point where we stop looking around and appreciating the simple things that are right in front of us. We drive home or walk through a city and can't even recall half the things we saw on the street. When you live off the land, you are forced to be hyper-aware of everything. I believe that achieving this level of hyperawareness makes people more complete because in addition to getting to know themselves better, they also develop a greater understanding of their relationships with other people.

While living on the land, everything becomes critical. If you don't pay attention, then you die. It sounds dramatic, but it's that simple. Being out in the wild strips away the artifice so that when you reenter society, you don't have the same distractions. I find that when I'm talking to a friend, I am immersed in their story and give them my full attention rather than worrying about who is texting me. (Yes, I do own a cell phone.)

Being in a survival situation teaches you what it takes to live. That connection is very powerful. All your senses become more developed. You experience heightened hearing and clearer eyesight. It can be highly addictive. When you live in such a way, you realize the potential of what you can be as a human being on a physical level, and it makes you want to return for more.

I see this pull in students I take on survival courses. We will go out for a month, and they will develop themselves in ways they have never experienced. Sometimes they push themselves so hard they feel enlightenment, but at the same time, they are craving a cheeseburger and an ice cream sandwich. They return to their city lives and get all those things they were dreaming about on the trail, but when they lose that wilderness boost, they return for more.

When you realize what the wild can do for you, there is a desire to mesh it with the modern world, even if you are not going to quit your job and become a hunter-gatherer. We know what nature can do for people who live in urban environments. We know it can build their awareness, their physicality, and their senses, and all of these can be adapted into their everyday lives. In our society today, the earth underneath us has become a distant thing. Most of us live in a concrete world removed from the true ground. I want to help people step off the concrete and onto the land.

So let's take a journey. Enjoy the land with me as I take you on a walkabout through the Southwest. See the celestial light bounce off the mountain. Relish the calm of nature's caves. Sweat it out when a mountain lion circles my tent in the night. Feel the pain of climbing out of the Grand Canyon in three feet of snow. Experience the rush of running the entire state of California. Stop to smell the roses and eat them, too—the rose hips, that is. Learn how nature mediates and sustains life.

Know all along that this journey is a true story. It may have happened yesterday, or it may have happened a thousand years ago. No matter. Being intimate with the land carries the same context. When we leave home and travel by foot, the soles of our feet find new treasures, as do the souls of our bodies.

EPIC SURVIVAL RULE #1:

SET YOUR OWN PATH

I am going to take the necessary steps to learn to fully live off the land. I want to live the way the American Indians did, and possibly even like our earliest ancestors in an even more primitive style. I am going to find a way to be closer to the earth and give the planet more than I take from it. On the surface, in a modern industrial society this doesn't seem possible, but I am going to try to show that it is.

The easiest starting point, it seems, is to find a way to slowly strip everything down to a bare minimum. This will allow me to reach the point where I can go out and see my direct impact on the land by foraging in an area without destroying the earth.

Most people are constantly beating up the earth and taking from the land. They are commuting to work in cars or on buses, producing reams of trash, and depleting natural resources just by living their lives. Almost no one is doing this maliciously. There is just simply no way around it.

To me, it appears that the earth is slowly dying and constantly, though fruitlessly, trying to replenish itself from man's impact on it. I am going to leave a gentler footprint, but I am going to do this for myself.

In this process, I am not going to judge other people who live differently than me. Not judging people is difficult, but it is a lesson that applies to anyone's life. You think you know something, you pass judgment on that, but then you later realize you didn't really know it.

I am attracted to the wilderness because it is a place where

I will be able to constantly learn how much I don't know. I am going to find a spiritual connection as well. I have no illusions that this will happen quickly. This is going to take years to understand. But I know I will succeed, because I am willing to risk my life in the process.

Chapter One

A GOLDEN SUNRISE

I was lying on a mountain ledge adjacent to Clouds Rest, a thin ridge of granite rising some four thousand feet above the Yosemite Valley and more than nine thousand feet above sea level. Darkness had set in. Snow was piling up. I hoped that the final fifty feet I had climbed to a small plateau the size of a park bench would be enough to keep the bears away from me during the night.

I was here because of a loosely related chain of events that made my path in life seem clear to me. At age seven, my parents separated. My mom and I moved around a lot, changing apartments once a year. When I was sixteen, we moved in with a man my mom was dating. His place was forty-five minutes away from my school. The distance, coupled with my lack of interest in classroom work, was the reason formal education began to fade from my life.

I never fit in with the traditional educational system. I was ridiculously motivated to learn, but I felt like school had me sitting in a chair eight hours a day, spending only one hour a day running around outside playing games. That was out of balance. I needed half my time to be outdoors, and though I didn't know it yet, I needed a large portion of the outdoor time to be nature based. Over time, it became not enough for me to be swinging a wooden club at a ball and running around a diamond and touching squares. I needed to experience the circles and ovals of nature.

Sitting at my desk in school, I would envision the natural world, just to keep my mind from feeling boxed in. I wasn't designed to sit and absorb information. In every school I attended, I was considered the best athlete. God gave me the gift to be fast and powerful, as well as light and swift. But when I sat in a classroom for eight hours a day, I was fighting against my natural gifts.

The turning point came early, in second grade. We opened up our history books to a chapter on Native Americans. To this day, I remember seeing a picture of a beautiful spear point. My heart immediately felt something. Though I couldn't articulate it then, I knew that the person who created that perfectly flinted spear point was somehow special. It was nothing like the tools I had seen in hardware stores; it had soul.

As I was marveling at this creation, my teacher told the class that we were also going to study their spiritual beliefs, but cautioned us that they "didn't know God like we do." Her telling the class that the Native Americans were lesser in the eyes of God made me instantly more attracted to them, because I knew there was more to that than the religious dogma they taught in parochial school.

The more the natural world came into view, the more I pulled away from school. Like most boys, I loved superheroes. Superman was cool, but it was Tarzan who captured my imagination, because he lived in the wild and protected both the people and the jungle itself. I was in awe of his physical attributes and how he lived as one with the world around him.

I wanted to be Tarzan, though I wasn't quite sure how to achieve that.

I felt a strong pull toward the lifestyle I was exposed to in my childhood at our cabin in Lake Arrowhead. My father was an avid amateur naturalist, and he taught me about plants and the smells of the trees and took me quail hunting. He took me on hikes. He would show me the land features and make me smell the plants. Most kids would probably think that was stupid and want to get on with the climb. I, however, immediately felt a connection to the natural world.

Between these experiences and my mother taking me to the beach on the weekends during the school year, I became captivated by how alive I felt in nature. Whether I was in the mountains or the city park, I felt different from when I was on pavement or in a building.

I often found people confusing, but nature always made sense to me.

When I turned seventeen, I took advantage of my parents' allowing me to make my own choices and moved to Yosemite. It was an ideal age to begin studying the wilderness. I had the strength of youth, no family relying on me, and years to explore on my terms. I arrived in the late fall. I took a job working at an ice cream store there. When it closed for the season, I worked in a cafeteria for another six weeks. I was a model employee, so I was chosen to work special functions and catered events. The best part about the job was that I only worked two days a week.

That freed me up to explore the land.

It also led to my being near the top of Clouds Rest during the biggest snowstorm of the winter, with only bears as my neighbors. But something unexpected happened on the mountain ledge: I didn't feel trapped. I felt free. As much as I was there because I wanted to be there, I was also there because I had to be there. I had climbed Clouds Rest because I knew there was something up there.

It was bigger than me, and I had to experience it.

In Yosemite at the time, backpacking was all the rage. On days off and weekends, young people who lived and worked in the area would go on overnight campouts. To me, those trips seemed like no more than tourist outings. I wanted my first backpacking trip to be off the charts and slightly insane, which is why I chose to climb Clouds Rest.

It was winter, and I was off work for a three-day weekend. There was snow on the ground and the temperature ranged from a high of forty in the day to the single digits at night. I put on shorts, socks and shoes, and a medium-weight fleece. To allow me to move at a rapid clip, I didn't bring a lot of supplies. I had a bivy sack—a lightweight, waterproof cover—to sleep inside of and help ward off the elements.

My goal was to climb Clouds Rest and then proceed across Half Dome. I wanted to spend the weekend up there with as few provisions as possible, and see what the land offered me.

The summit of Half Dome was once thought to be impossible to reach. In 1870, a report called it "probably the only one of all the prominent points about the Yosemite which has never been, and never will be, trodden by human foot." Five years later, climber George Anderson, who was laying the cable route that climbers now use, accessed it. More than a hundred years after that, any climber in good physical condition is able to reach the summit.

People I worked with had cautioned me that Clouds Rest was too treacherous a climb and the wintry conditions were too brutal for my first long backpacking trip, particularly since I was going it alone—and in shorts! But I had to see it.

I pretty much ran up the mountain. As I was going up, a snowstorm was starting to blanket the land. About seven miles up, I reached a halfway point where people climbing Half Dome set up their base camps. The area was emptying out. Hikers were coming off the mountain and heading back to town. Every person I passed warned me that the storm was already outrageous and getting worse, which only made me want to go even higher.

Something was driving me to get up there and see what it looked like in the thick of the storm.

I continued past Little Yosemite Valley toward Clouds Rest. The trees started to thin out, and soon I was above the tree line. I reached a point about two miles from the peak. The land was pure white. The snow was getting thicker and thicker, and the visibility was about five feet. Because I was moving fast, I wasn't cold, despite the fact that I was wearing shorts.

Still, I had to continue climbing. I was feeling drawn. Though most people would feel that I was entering a dangerous situation, I wasn't scared or concerned for my safety. This was not a foolish ego trip. In fact, there was no ego involved. I was doing this for myself. I knew that as long as I made the right decisions along the way, I would not get hurt. I would not cross the line to where things became too dangerous. Fear would not become a factor.

Everybody has a certain way they approach and handle fear. I believe that people who are on a genuine path and are being true to themselves as well as everything around them can ward off fear. The situation is never just about us. There is a greater force that is pulling us to what we should be doing.

Knowing you are on the right life path can mitigate fear.

Some degree of fear can be appropriate and healthy. It can compel you to make sane decisions rather than rash ones. But fear creeps in and becomes dangerous when you are doing something you should not be doing. Uncontrollable fear occurs when you are in the wrong place at the wrong time and you are caught off guard. You have either arrived in the wrong place to begin with, or you have undertaken the wrong course of action. In that situation, we lose the ability to control our fear.

So there I was: The storm was packed with energy. With every step, the snow became thicker. It soon reached the point of a whiteout. Even though the peak of Half Dome was directly ahead of me, I couldn't see it. I was moving by simply feeling the land. If I detected a cliff, I turned and went in a different direction.

Eventually I hit a rock wall that stopped me. I stood still and tried to let the land tell me what to do. Every once in a while, a beam of light would break through the thick snow. From what I could see, it looked like there was a small peak directly in front of me, about fifty feet up a rock wall.

The sheer newness of the area was captivating. What was up there? For the excitement of what I might find, I decided to climb the snow-covered face of the wall. The climb turned out to be easier than it appeared to be because the wall was smaller than I had imagined.

The plateau at the top of the wall was roughly three by six feet. I tried to look down the other side, which would normally provide a sweeping view of Yosemite Valley, but the visibility was zero. I was walled in by blowing snow. I assumed the cliff in front of me was probably steeper than the cliff I had climbed, but there was no way to know for sure until the snow stopped.

I decided to spend the night there. Though the area was known for bears, I wasn't worried about bears coming for my food. I knew—or rather I had been told—that a bear couldn't climb a near-ninety-degree rock wall.

The snow was falling in thick sheets and the wind was picking up. I pulled out my body bag and my bivy sack and crawled into them. I lay there, not afraid but intensely curious about what the storm would do to me.

It was my first test of patience in the wild. I would have to wait out a night—or maybe longer—on this peak. I would have to appreciate and respect the energy of the massive storm. I didn't sleep a wink. The wind was way too intense. Throughout the night, as huge gusts blasted me, I curled up tighter and tighter into a ball. I was completely drenched. The body bag seemed to do nothing to protect me.

Because I had a Christian upbringing, I found myself praying throughout the night, not for my safety but for a gift.

During the night, during the storm, I received it.

Though I was lying near the top of Clouds Rest, wet and cold, covered by what felt like an iced towel, the excitement kept me warm. I had a feeling something was going to happen. I didn't know what. I wasn't the least bit afraid, because I was waiting for something extraordinary. I thought maybe the peak would break loose and float away.

At some point just before dawn, after being awake all night, I managed to fall asleep.

When I opened my eyes, I learned how Clouds Rest had gotten its name. The sunlight was shining on my face. I lifted my head and looked out over a crisp blue sky. At the exact same level of the peak where I was lying was a layer of clouds that went on forever. I was just above the cloud line, so I couldn't see anything below. It looked like I could step out and walk across the layer of clouds.

Actually, I thought about trying.

Still to this day, I have never seen such a sight in the mountains, or in an airplane descending through clouds, for that matter. Those clouds provided a perfect floor for the sky, much the way the land does for mountains.

I sat up and watched the sun rise. It was a magical sight. As the sun crested the horizon, the entire cloud layer turned orange. It took about an hour for the sun to fully rise and the white color to return to the clouds. The sky was now clear. There was no sign of snow.

I imagined that this must be God's view of us and the sunrise.

I packed my wet belongings and descended from the clouds. At the base of the rock, where I had climbed up to sleep, there were fresh bear tracks. Clearly, a bear had been trying to get up onto the peak to eat my food. I never saw the bear, and I never feared that I might have been in danger. The bear couldn't have climbed the rock, because it was too steep for an animal with claws.

I came down the mountain without incident and without seeing any hikers, all of whom had been discouraged by the storm.

For my first climbing experience, I took what I had seen as a sign. I had the feeling of being given a gift. I had gone to a place where everybody told me not to go; yet despite their warnings, everything inside me told me that I needed to go there to see something. And I had.

I had been blessed with the sight of a magic carpet of clouds and an immediate sunrise that few humans ever see. It was a transformative experience that validated the unusual, nonacademic path I had chosen, and showed me that the natural world held unlimited possibilities.

Coming off that experience, I was elated. I felt so full of light. When I returned to the valley floor and tried to talk to people about what I had seen, I felt as though I was talking to a wall. In comparison, everything else seemed dull.

The contrast was so stark that I began to separate life in society, the artificial world, from life in the wilderness, the real world. I began to understand that if I made nature my sole study, I would always see the world through a different lens than people in society.

But I was ready and willing to take that journey.

Chapter Two

STRADDLING TWO WORLDS

There was a lateral drift to my life from my late teens leading into the precipice of adulthood at age twenty-one. I felt that the flexibility of moving to different areas and exploring them would lead to an education of the wild, and ultimately to a grounding. It was my version of backpacking through Europe to discover myself and decide what kind of life I would lead.

I lived one winter in Mammoth Lakes. I found a job at a ski shop and spent my spare time hiking in the backcountry. I entertained the thought of touring all the national parks and working for several months in each one. I even called around to the parks to see which jobs were available. I was offered a job as a tour boat guide in the Everglades National Park in South Florida. I almost accepted the job, but I ended up turning it down because in my mind I hadn't seen enough of the Sierras yet. The Sierras felt like my home, and I wanted to explore them.

I had arrived in Yosemite with preconceived judgments on people's relationship to the environment. I thought that people who didn't use paper bags, and instead brought reusable ones, when they went to the market were pretentious. In Yosemite, there was a lot of acting "green." It was the first time I was exposed to that mind-set.

But the land kicked me in the butt. It seemed to be saying that whether or not this behavior was fake, to that person they were taking a step to be a better steward of the land. It also taught me that I needed to find a way to practice the ideals of a more natural lifestyle in my own way.

At the moment I made that commitment, I felt a change inside me taking hold. As soon as I started studying primitive skills, I looked for everyday ways to stop destroying the earth. At the time, I was living in the Sequoia National Park. My diet was conducive to healthy living. I ate mostly rice, lentils, and wild greens. I never ate processed food of any kind, or anything with sugar in it.

I took a pledge not to set foot in a motor vehicle for eight months. I had always been rebellious toward automobiles and supported the view that many of our environmental problems would not exist without cars. Without motor vehicles, people would be forced to have a greater respect for the place they live, as there would be no quick escapes. Most people love their cars and all the voice-commanded gadgets in them, but how many people are interested in an interaction with their car's exhaust?

I still strongly believe that cars and motorized transportation, in addition to causing environmental harm, are responsible for a universal loss of health and fitness, as well as our society's overall sanity. Anytime we fight against the grain of nature, there is a price to be paid. As we balance the needs of our lives, we need to be wary of how much compromise we are willing to accept. Going back to nature is an attempt to reestablish ourselves, and people who don't do that end up unhappy with their lives. When people search and find that balance, it provides a certain amount of peace and sanity.

I actually tried to do something about the overuse of motor vehicles. When Bill Clinton was president, I wrote him a letter to advocate building more bike and running trails that actually go places. I proposed that these trails parallel roads and interstates and run through cities. To me, it seemed that we built these tight highways with no shoulder and no place for a person to ride a bike or want to walk, let alone even safely walk. If we could just lay woodchips along the roads, we would start creating more happiness in our lives. To add an element, we could make those trails cut off the highway so that bikers and pedestrians could pick up a bit of scenery.

Part of the problem is that in order to make everything practical and fast, society has sacrificed our artistry and our connection with nature. To me, those words go hand in hand. Nature, without even trying, is an artistic masterpiece, but when we interrupt that flow with skyscrapers and freeways, it disconnects us. If we can figure out how to interject things in our life that make us feel happy and connected, like walking through a beautiful spot, there will be a way to maintain that artistry in our life that breeds feelings of passion. Working within the confines of nature and not mowing down every tree acknowledges that we want to be part of that artistry.

As soon as I made my pledge to stay out of cars, I went on a three-day run. But instead of covering my typical twenty-five miles a day, I ran sixty-five miles a day. It was intense. I had never run that far before, or even close to that far. When I finally stopped, I actually sat down and prayed. I thanked God for giving me the strength and the body to cover such a distance. I thought that maybe he had given me such power because of the commitment I had made to improve the earth.

That thought resonated. Right after I had committed to not riding in a vehicle, I was given the stamina and strength to do something that most people could not, even if they were extremely fit. There had to be a connection, though I couldn't quantify it at the time. The one thing I did begin to feel was that running heightened my instincts for the terrain.

Socially, I must admit, living on foot was a challenge. When friends invited me to a party that was eight miles from my house, I jogged there. It also presented problems when I asked a girl out on a date. Even the most adventuresome women weren't willing to walk five miles to dinner. Though my friends admired me, they didn't fully understand why anyone would purposefully make their lives harder. I felt I was making it better.

I gained a reputation among the year-rounders in Sequoia as a distance runner. The Park Service became aware of my ability to cover long distances of terrain very quickly. After I worked a short stint in the reservations office, the Park Service asked me to join the search-and-rescue team. They used me for urgent distress calls that required an immediate reconnaissance on foot.

One afternoon, there was an extensive search-and-rescue mission for a lost teenager. He and a group of friends had been out for a day hike. He had left the group early, but he never made it back to town. The search was concentrated in the area where he had last been seen. Day one ended with no clues.

After the second day ended with no sign of his whereabouts, I studied maps of the area. I asked the ranger in charge if they had covered a certain area that was several miles from their primary search radius. He told me that the young man couldn't have made it that far in two days. I told him that I believed he could have made it much farther.

Generally, people who are lost first walk in circles trying to find their way out. But it was clear to me after the search team had spent two days covering the circle route that he had chosen a different path.

The route I had projected was downhill. Given a choice, most people will walk downhill rather than uphill when they are lost. As he traveled, the terrain would have become lusher and moister, meaning he would have thought water was nearby. Though this was logical, part of my instinct about his location came from my time running in the area, spending time covering that land, and understanding where he could naturally wander.

Four and a half days later, the teenager popped out on a road and was picked up by a passerby in the area where I had suggested they search.

The head ranger was impressed that I had pinpointed the missing teenager's location. My knowledge of the terrain, combined with my ability to run and my interest in tracking, resulted in him putting me on a "hasty crew." They are the first responders in a search, and they generally hike or run to the site. I was teamed with another physically fit ranger.

Weeks later, a report of another missing teenager came in. The teenager had been backpacking with a friend who had left the hike to return to work. The teenager was supposed to stay another two nights in the backcountry. Three days had passed with no word from him.

My colleague and I took off running up the trail. We zigzagged, covering the valley floor on our way to his last known location. En route, we came upon a waterfall that was about six miles away. I felt something as we passed through the area. I felt that the teenager was nearby. Part of my sense of his location came from reading the land, but just as much of it was a strong gut feeling.

The ranger was understandably skeptical. The location I pinpointed was far from the kid's last known location. He agreed to stop and let me have a few minutes to explore my hunch.

I didn't find any foot tracks, so I stopped reading the dirt and started reading the water. I stared at the nearby waterfall. In my head I began to form a picture of what felt like actual events.

Okay . . . if somebody came down that waterfall a quarter mile upstream and they were unconscious, where would they end up? Downstream somewhere. Perhaps caught under that large rock.

I walked downstream and stood on the rock. Instantly, I had a sharp pain in my gut that felt like my appendix had burst. I made my way across the boulders to the other side to try to look under the rock. The other ranger was watching me, somewhat bewildered.

I was trying to establish a position to look under the rock. There was a strong current flowing downstream that obstructed my ability to see below the surface of the water. I looked from several different angles, but I couldn't make out anything that looked like a body. Then I started to take off my shirt.

"Can I go in?" I yelled up to my colleague.

"That's not your job," he said. "If you see something, we need to call in the dive crew."

"I don't see anything," I said. "I just *feel* like something is under there."

We exchanged a few more words, and he insisted that we call in the divers.

I again cautioned him that it was just a hunch. I was twenty-one. I wasn't an expert tracker by any means. I had been on the job for only a few weeks, and I didn't want to be responsible for wasting resources on a hunch.

Even if he doubted me, the ranger had watched me closely enough to know there was a possibility, remote as it might have been, that I might be right. We also had nothing else to go on. He called for the dive crew.

Hours later, the divers found the young man's body under the rock I had pinpointed.

The debrief was a solemn affair, but the head ranger was very firm about his belief in my abilities. "I've been on a lot of searches," he told the group. "I'm a trained tracker. I have no idea what led Matt to think there was a body under there. The only possible way is that he has a psychic ability. Without Matt, we never would have found this body. For that we are grateful. We would have spent two weeks with no results and probably a million dollars on the search."

The fact is, they never would have found the body because they were searching six miles away. The land was untrackable. Where we started out, it was pine-needled forest with a little dirt here and there. But above the waterfall, it was 100 percent granite. It takes a highly skilled tracker to track on rock, and the ranger service didn't have such a tracker.

I offered to speak to the teenager's parents, but the head ranger told me it was best to handle things through formal channels. "You've helped bring closure for the family," he said. "Remember that."

The season ended in October without any further serious incidents. We had two more fairly basic rescues in the ensuing seven months, but nothing near a casualty. I finished out the season on the search-and-rescue team—on foot.

I felt like it was time to move on. I wanted to explore the backcountry. I owned only about twenty pounds of gear. I had a sleeping bag, a bivy sack, a couple changes of clothes, a few pairs of handmade sandals, and some maps. I modified a pair of running shoes into sandals to alternate wearing with my sandals, because they would provide more cover for my feet in the snow. I loaded everything into my backpack and took off running to the east toward the Sierra Nevada mountain range.

I didn't have a destination in my mind.

The day I set out there was an early-season, blinding snowstorm. The visibility was less than ten feet. But when I reached the mountains, a path of blue sky emerged and seemed to guide me as I made my way over the pass.

I first stopped in Kern River Canyon, a wonderful valley that the naturalist John Muir loved. I ran into the north fork. This particular valley remains one of my favorite spots on earth. From there, I could see Mount Whitney, the largest peak in the lower States, which towers some 14,505 feet above the valley. The entire bowl surrounds the upper part of the valley and drains into it, so there are magical waterfalls bordering all sides.

One of Muir's favorite spots was the hot springs. I had previously been there a couple times. For a hiker, it is reachable with a decent amount of endurance and some know-how. But because it's a forty-mile walk from the closest drop-off point, you almost always have the place to yourself.

I stayed there for four days, recovering and regrouping. I relaxed in the hot springs, made teas, collected plants, and fished. I loved making tea out of the needles from the pine trees. I am convinced that it's one of the healthiest teas there is. You take the pine needles and smash them up into a pulp and drop that into boiling water. If you drink it often, the antioxidants in this tea will add years to your life.

One day while walking through the area, I met a random guy. He said he was camping in the lower valley and had hiked to the hot springs. I asked him how long he had been in the area. When he told me he had been out for four weeks, I only half believed him. He didn't look like the type who could stay out there long. He looked like an average city businessman.

It turned out he was a producer of Budweiser commercials—or at least that's what he told me. He said the reason he was able to stay out so long was that he was having a helicopter bring him supplies. Where I was camped that wouldn't have been possible, but based on where he was camped, the story seemed legitimate. He was on the border of the park and the forest, so a helicopter would be able to land there.

I spent a night there. We shared a campfire and talked a little bit. It was mostly small talk. He kept rambling on about the Bud commercials he had done and the different location shoots. He saw the land from a completely different point of view than me. We were both looking at the same water falling down the granite face of the mountain, but he was interpreting its value differently. I saw the small things the waterfall produced and fed, like the streams and the wildlife. To him, it was a backdrop for a beer commercial.

He told me I should be in a commercial because I had a "rough and worn look." I gave him my parents' phone number. Of course, after we parted company the following morning, I never heard from him or saw him again.

I stayed in the hot springs area for about a week. I then started hiking south, following the length of the range of the Sierras.

The Sierras are a monocline that runs north–south. The east side is steep, while the west side has a more gradual descent. On the east side, if you were to take a hiking trail up, it would be about fifteen miles to the ridge. If you were to take a hiking trail from the west side, you would be looking at more like fifty miles to that same ridge. I followed the north–south ridge for eighty miles, all the way until the Sierras tapered out at the foot of the Mojave Desert, which almost curls around them.

When I came down out of the mountains, I stopped in a small town called Tehachapi. In total, my journey had been about 130 miles. The walk over the Sierras was a nice way to cap off the months I had spent living on foot and not riding in a motorized vehicle.

There, I ended my goal of not setting foot in a car the old-fashioned way: I put out my thumb and hitchhiked back to my mom's house in Huntington Beach.

Chapter Three

ON MY TERMS

I found myself torn. I had set myself on an unusual path in life. But I was still young, and I felt as if I needed to reground myself in the real world. It wasn't about making money. In my life, money was for wants; it wasn't for needs. It was more a sense of trying to feel like I belonged to something concrete, so to speak.

During my walk through the Sierras, I admit that I felt lonely at times. I loved what I was learning in the wilderness, and how the wilds responded to me and I to them. But I also missed the ease of the city and being with my friends. I didn't want to be forced to choose one life or the other. I wanted to take the best of both worlds, but I wasn't really sure how to, or even if it was possible.

I ended up staying in the Huntington Beach area that winter and working for my dad. He owned a construction company that had a contract with the aerospace manufacturing company McDonnell Douglas. Life there wasn't all steel and concrete. I was near the ocean, where I could surf again. I was also back where I had grown up.

The working life wasn't completely foreign to me. I never had any trouble finding a job. People liked me, and I had a determination and dedication that showed. Employers were attracted to that, but I wanted to push away from normal jobs.

As I tried to relate to the people I had grown up with who had gotten married and had full-time jobs, I recognized that everybody's life is different. The phases are what allow someone to be a loner and not be alone. At that age, I was still developing and maturing as a person. I wanted to interact in a community and have friends, which made it harder to be alone.

Being alone is rewarding if you connect to the land, because what you get out of it is amazing. The plants and animals don't literally talk to you, but they almost do. There is nothing you can do to replace those experiences. When you are alone in the wilderness, you are struggling hard to understand something deeper, but nobody is there to help you. Ultimately, even the strongest people are going to feel a sense of loneliness.

The mental fortitude and patience it takes to be alone are way beyond what most people are capable of. Though I knew I was able to live alone, I didn't have the patience or mental strength at that age to be alone for significant periods of time.

I found that when I talked about being alone, most people could only conceptualize that as sitting on their couch watching TV and eating food. That has nothing to do with being alone. Even reading a book is not being alone because you inhabit someone else's illusionary world.

But being alone in the wilderness is something else entirely. There is no escape. You must be immersed and present with everything that is going on around you. Being back in society, I saw that people had created the ability to escape from the moment in different ways. While that makes life easier for that moment because it allows people to check out of reality, it also destroys our ability to be patient and present.

It helped that I didn't own anything, so I had nothing to come back to. All my belongings could fit in a backpack or tote bag. If it did not fit into my backpack, I gave it away. My only real connections were with friends or directly with the land, so for me to wander off on my own was easy. Yet I was still conflicted.

My experiences in the wilderness were giving me some deeper perspectives that others could not understand, nor could I fully. I appreciated the newfound and profound wisdom I was gaining, but I also began to feel a distance from people. To those around me, it seemed that I wanted to be a "hermit rather than a cool guy," as one guy put it. I also noticed that I had fewer close friendships and a harder time relating to people on everyday issues.

I found that for some, the phrase *living off the land* meant living "simple" and "lacking intelligence." I had discovered that this could not be farther from the truth. There is nothing simple about living off the land. It requires innate and learned intelligence to adjust to the natural changes around you—otherwise you will not survive. There is also evidence that the hunter-gatherer lifestyle stimulates psychological and physical well-being by returning us to the land, making it one of the most complex and invigorating ways to live.

It has been suggested that the cures to many modern ills can be found in natural living. The renowned naturalist and ecologist Paul Shepard conducted some of the definitive studies on early nature-based cultures. He concluded that humans, who over the millennia have spent nearly all of their social history in hunting-and-gathering environments, must be close to nature to properly grow emotionally and psychologically.

Shepard determined that the shift over our hundreds of thousands of years from hunter-gatherers to settled agriculturalists destroyed not only our surroundings but also us. Bucking our innate desire for the wilderness has taken us out of our natural element and as a result created many of the psychological and physical problems that exist today.

The one thing I knew was that I did not want to give up my enriching experiences in the wild just to be more relatable at a party. It was at that point that I decided I should not turn my back on the wisdom that nature was offering that could help others; rather I should further explore this call at whatever personal cost. I reached the conclusion that I would have to become a better communicator with the forest in order to explain and teach others the language of the earth. I made it a goal to figure out a way to bring friends and others to terms with the wilderness.

Before returning to Huntington Beach, I had walked virtually everywhere I went. I covered not just the length of California but also many of its nooks and crannies. I would meet people everywhere I went. But when I looked at them, I felt that they were boxed in and had lost their freedom. I didn't want to be like that. I didn't want to lose my freedom. I regarded these people as unhealthy, because they were trapped in a system that degraded their minds and their health. It scared me. I promised myself I would never fall into that trap.

For me, a large part of living off the land alone in the wilderness was not destroying or taking anything from the earth. Growing up, Christianity had taught me about being kind to people. But I had concluded that it wasn't enough to be kind to people while beating up the earth. To avoid falling into that trap, I kept my possessions to a minimum. I had seen friends in my field with ties to material things, and I could see it was pulling them away from the wilderness. That aspect scared me as well.

The other struggle I had was trying to share what I had learned. I felt that I was getting to a point where I could live off the land and not destroy the earth. But being back in society, it looked like everybody else was destroying the earth. I began to question what good I, as one person, could do if I slipped away and back into that lifestyle. Asking these questions resulted in me acknowledging that there was more to my life than just my relationship with the wilderness. I had to include other people's relationships with the wilderness.

One of the most important things I had learned from living off the land is to be more observant. I saw that my friends would drive home or walk around Huntington Beach and not even recall what they saw. Living off the land made me aware of everything. In addition to helping me know myself better, it also led me to pay closer attention to people.

I was careful not to be preachy. I tried to live by example. If asked, I would gladly share my love for the wilderness and my stories with people who wanted to hear them. But I focused on living by example. I knew that I could never convince somebody in a dialogue. I never dictated to others. Even though I was searching for answers, I never judged anyone else's life. I was arriving at my own conclusion on what was a kinder way to live. It was working for me. I was hopeful it would work for others if they chose to look for it. But at the same time, I felt a certain amount of confusion that so few people chose to live that way. Because more people weren't pursuing my chosen lifestyle, it made me constantly question what was wrong with it.

At some point, as I was rounding out my skills and filling out the full picture, I started leaning harder on the life of a survivalist. I was constantly pushing myself and riding a fine line. I would run sixty-five miles in a day from Death Valley to the Sierras. Every few months, I would sit on a mountaintop and fast for one full cycle of a day and two nights. I would run barefoot in the snow. Instead of sleeping on a bed when I was in civilization, I chose to sleep on a wooden board to harden my bones and my body. I would purposefully bathe under icy water in the wintertime.

Ultimately, that is what created the deeper connection for me and made me come to the realization that the wilderness would be my life's path. My intentions were pure. I believed in what I was doing so strongly that I was willing to die for it. But at the same time, I believed that the wilderness saw my intentions and therefore wasn't going to kill me.

EPIC SURVIVAL RULE #2:

BE PHYSICALLY IN CONTROL

*Because I don't own a car, I am going to focus on three phys-
ical elements to cover the landscape: running, climbing, and
swimming. I believe that if I can master those three natural
modes of transportation, I can travel anywhere I want go.*

*Swimming is important to me because I grew up near the
ocean, and I love to go on long-distance ocean swims. I use
swimming as a relief from the heat. I also know that there will
be times when crossing to safety requires me to swim across
a body of water.*

*Climbing is critical because the earth is not flat. If I do not
learn to scale a steep rock properly, I am putting myself in danger every time I move across the land. I will need to climb to
cross mountain ranges. I will also need to climb to find a perch
where I can avoid animals coming after my food at night.*

*Running is the most important means of transporting my-
self from one place to the next. It is my primary means of exploring new areas. It also allows me to speed up the basic
tasks of living in the wild, like hunting for food or seeking shelter in threatening weather.*

*At the same time that I need to be strong in these areas, I
am also starting to realize that no matter how physically developed I become, I cannot compete against nature. The wild will
destroy me if I try to compete against it. I can't throw myself off
a cliff and expect to pop up like a rubber ball, nor can I jump
into a flash flood and survive.*

I also see that it is futile to compete against the wild. Why would I want to go out and do battle with something that is so real, so beautiful, and so much a part of me? That defeats the point of being out in the wild.

However, the dilemma remains that at the same time nature is beautiful, it is fierce. That scares people. That ferocity keeps our awareness intact. I know that if I use my fitness to exist in that fierceness rather than fighting against it, I will be protected.

Chapter Four

"MUSCLE-HEAD MATT"

I was terrified of heights. That fear had been instilled in me by vague memories of working in a circus and falling to my death. I don't know what those memories mean, or where they came from. Some people attribute such things to reincarnation. I'm not sure that is the case, but in any event they were recurring thoughts. I knew that to be able to fully connect with the land and be able to live as a hunter-gatherer I would need to overcome my fear of heights and become a proficient climber.

The physical aspects of climbing appealed to me. I hoped to use those to placate my fears. I grew up as an athlete and led a very physical life. When I saw climbers, I noticed they always had good physiques. I thought, *I want to look that fit.*

While those were the initial reasons I invested myself in climbing, they would soon fade into the background. Climbing became less about me and more about the art of climbing itself. It became about a dance or a meditation with the rock, about how to listen to and move with the land in the way it dictates, and about how not to force my physicality on the rock.

Learning about climbing was more of a mental process than a physical one. The only formal instruction I had was a beginner-level climbing class at a mountaineer school. I was taught basic rope work and a few safety precautions. Following that one class, I would just show up in the valley, where there were enough climbers to help show me the ropes, so to speak.

When I first started climbing, I was such an accomplished athlete that I could just muscle my way up the rock. I attacked the rock like it was a physical challenge, such as bench pressing my body weight or sprinting a lap around a track. I was a *yarder*, the term used for people who pull overly hard with their arms. My ferocity and overall lack of grace on the rock caused the climbers to give me the embarrassing nickname "Muscle-Head Matt."

As challenging as making it up the rock was, I now had another obstacle to overcome.

In my early climbing days, I had several white-knuckle incidents. Most of them came when I wasn't climbing with a rope. They were soloing or scrambling experiences.

My first close brush with death was when my friend Jake and I hiked up to the top of El Capitan, the largest monolith of granite rock in the world. Experienced climbers from all over the world travel to Yosemite to tackle the three-thousand-plus-foot climb. After we made it up the trail, we decided not to hike back down the same way. Instead, we opted for a steep gully on the right side the trail.

The gully descended the full three thousand feet. From a technical standpoint, it was extremely dangerous. The rock was also very chalky and loose, which made it over-the-top dangerous. We also both had backpacks, giving us extra weight that increased the difficulty.

At one point, I was climbing down a big flake—a rock sheet that juts out on its own. I was holding on tightly. Jake was below me. His climbing technique was far more accomplished than mine. I was still muscling everything. Jake was using his feet to work his way down the rock, while I was using my arms, yarding on the flake.

Without a sound or any other warning, the flake snapped. A thin chunk of stone broke off in my hands, leaving me in a free fall. I went flying through the air, still grasping the stone. Instinctively, I let go of the stone to free my hands.

I continued to fall straight down the vertical rock about twenty-five feet until my backpack slammed down on a rock. I hit so hard it felt like I scrambled my internal organs. The impact flipped me. I hit the ground in a slightly sloped area and began sliding down the hill.

Frantically, I grabbed at rocks and trees to stop my slide. I managed to latch on to the base of a tree seconds before I fell off a two-hundred-foot drop. I hung there with my arms wrapped desperately around the tree, half my body on the rock and the other half dangling over the edge. I was a hundred feet below Jake.

"Are you okay?" Jake yelled. "Are you stable?"

I told him I was.

"Man, I saw you flip off that rock and I thought you were done," he said, summing up the fall.

So did I. I pulled myself back up onto the rock. It was my first real climbing lesson. The rock was warning me that I needed to become a more graceful climber. Jake was below me, and I could have very easily hit him with part of the broken flake.

And if I don't grab that tree, I die.

The near-death experience rattled me, but it also motivated me. My first thought was that I wouldn't climb chalky rock. Unfortunately, where

I lived, there was always going to be chalky rock. I needed to learn to climb it properly.

I fully realized that I would not be a true climber until I improved my technique and established some finesse. I also knew that I needed to find them on my own, not in climbing school.

I began studying the rocks. I would go out to the base and stare up at a rock for hours and hours. I wanted to establish an appreciation for the rock. These cliffs were an integral part of the earth, not climbing walls with plastic notches dragged behind pickup trucks to carnivals. The rocks had been carved and honed by Mother Nature over millions of years. I had to learn to respect them.

I also decided to climb easier rocks without a rope to learn how to move on the stone. This allowed me to stop being afraid that I wouldn't make it up the rock. During this time, I started to enjoy how the rock carried me over it. Once I felt that connection, I began to see climbing as a graceful dance that nature was teaching me, rather than as a man battling the elements to survive.

My technique needed improvement. I had to learn to distribute my weight more evenly and move the way the rock wanted me to move on it. Once I altered my technique, I started to feel like I was connecting with the rock. I started moving with the rock in a way that the land wanted me to move. It felt as if I were dancing on the rock. I could almost envision the rock gods and the tree gods looking up and saying, "I really appreciate how that guy is climbing."

Oddly, when you reach that point, in some ways it feels like you are giving something back to nature. Every aspect of the land is giving and receiving energy—all the rocks, all the animals, everything.

Let's say a climber makes his way up a rock crack. There are chipmunks frolicking and plants flourishing. The chipmunks communicate with their chirping and movements as they jockey for position for food. Plants have different ways of communicating that we don't fully understand.

Now let's say a climber brings a boom box and plays some heavy-metal music. Then he starts yarding on the rock. His rough climbing pulls a bunch of loose rock down, but he doesn't care. He keeps going. Maybe he steps on a loose boulder that rolls down the crack. During this process, he might have disrupted a squirrel house or even an unseen endangered falcon's nest. Even if there is no visible damage, he is certainly freaking out all of the animals and disrupting that whole area. Of course, he didn't realize that because he was not paying attention.

But if a climber goes up there and climbs with focus, attention, and purpose, even a hawk or a golden eagle that has lived on the land its entire life will fly by and appreciate the way he is moving on that piece of rock. Seeing that climber might just make the hawk's day. It lives there. It is part of the land, so in essence, the climber is giving something back simply by climbing well, as strange as that may sound.

I found this to be true. When I started climbing with finesse, hawks always came to watch me. When I sucked, I never saw a bird anywhere near me.

Of course, there's no way to know when you reach that level. There's not a light that goes off, or a special call you hear from the hawks. The only tangible way would be if a spectator were to look up and say, "That guy is moving gracefully up the rock, rather than fighting to get to the top without falling." What it comes down to is the difference between a person who has a strong intention and one who does not.

Intent is a powerful driver. Whenever I travel across the land, I will always connect with the native people. They will look at me and say, "Strong heart." What they are seeing is not a guy who can know everything and live off their land. The native people can feel when somebody has an awareness of and an intention to learn their land. That intent can be extended to anything in the wild.

About a year after I began climbing, one of the world's greatest climbers Peter Croft, showed up to watch me on several occasions. From high up on the rock, I would look down and see Peter staring at me. I wondered if he thought I was going to die because I was a hundred feet up without a rope. He would spend hours watching me, but by the time I descended, he was always gone.

I knew from other climbers that Peter was shy. One day, I bumped into his wife in town and asked her why he was watching me. "He loves to watch you climb because you climb like you appreciate and love the rock," she said.

That was huge for me. I had gone from "Muscle-Head Matt" to being appreciated by a world-renowned free climber. It validated that I had a connection to the rock, and that I could make the connection stronger if I looked and listened, instead of trying to battle the land.

I had come to realize that when you put up your defenses and try to battle something, you don't get very far, but if you work with something, be it the land or people, you get a better experience—even if that inter-action is with an immovable force. When you watch the best climbers on the hardest climbs, you won't notice how difficult it is unless they fall. They maintain their grace and cool until the moment they pop off the rock. It's the inexperienced climber that is grunting, grasping, battling, not moving well, and losing all technique and focus—and probably not getting up the rock. It looks like a schizophrenic spider trying to figure out where to go, darting in one direction, then another.

The process of climbing is like a jigsaw puzzle. You look up the rock ten to thirteen feet and mentally measure your moves. You think, what's the sequence? Where do I put my hand? I see a geological pocket in the stone caused by some type of organic vegetation that was trapped and has decayed. Does it look too soft? If so, then you shorten your moves until you can test the spots.

But the danger never disappears. Even after I became a confident climber, I had close calls. The first was when I was free soloing—climbing without a rope—Half Dome in Yosemite. Having been there on my first backpacking expedition, I knew there was an easy route on the south side that wasn't directly on the face. It was a big crystal dyke that went up for a couple thousand feet. I climbed the first four hundred feet or so and hit the critical juncture.

I knew from reading the guidebook that this move was the crux of the whole climb. You had to move along a polish (a rock ledge) for about eight feet before you reconnected with the dyke. When you use a rope, you clip in at that point so if you fall, you can swing over to the dyke. Without a rope, that move was dicier than most five- to six-rated moves, which was the rating of the climb.

I stopped and worked out the move in my head. Mentally, I saw it. But then I checked the footing. It was very unstable. I concluded the risk was not worth it. I climbed back down the dyke, descending the four hundred feet I'd climbed up, to the bottom.

Unsatisfied with my climb, I decided to take a more challenging way to the base. Instead of hiking back to the trail, I went down the face on an edge where there was a ravine. I had to climb down the ravine backward because it was so steep. The ground was loose. In some regard, it was reminiscent of the El Cap adventure, but technically much harder.

When I got about halfway down, I felt that I was in the clear. I then spotted a rope coming off the face. The long, static line was about a thousand feet. It came down off the face and disappeared into the ravine. The terrain was becoming increasingly steeper so I decided to use the rope as backup, as a sort of guide line. I put my hand on the rope and continued the downward moves.

After a few steps, the granite under my feet turned to loose ball bearings. The footing was so poor I started sliding. I grabbed the rope firmly with my right hand. I was now using it for support. Trouble was, a thousand feet of rope has a lot of stretch in it, so I was holding on but continuing to slide down the ravine.

After about twenty-five feet I could feel the rope getting tighter and tighter. Then it became so taut that I gripped it with my other hand. When it tightened fully, I had all my weight on it. But the rope was so long and I put so much force on it that it turned into a rubber band and popped me up out of the ravine.

I was literally flying across the face of Half Dome, Tarzan-style, some five hundred feet off the floor. To avoid crashing into the rock, I pushed off with my feet. Now I was free swinging out over the rock, doing a hundred-foot pendulum. I was desperately looking around, trying to determine where I could land. There wasn't a person in sight.

As I was swinging back and forth, I realized that the rope wasn't long enough for me to reach the bottom. I was stuck on a sheer face of Half Dome.

I spotted a dihedral, which is an inside corner of rock. I could see that it had a plateau on top and thought that maybe I could make it up to the plateau to get my bearings. But that escape plan was fleeting. I quickly realized the rope wasn't swinging me to the plateau; it was swinging me into a rock crack about thirty feet below the plateau.

I hit the crack hard, did a quick hand jam into it, and wedged myself in. I lifted my feet and stuck them in the crack so I could regroup and assess the easiest way down. I checked the rope's length again, but determined it wouldn't reach the bottom.

I looked up and saw that the plateau was only about thirty feet above me, in what appeared to be an easy climb. As a backup plan, I wedged the rope into the crack in case I needed it later. I then started free soloing. I was four hundred feet off the deck, doing this very difficult crack (rated 5.8, a fairly challenging climb for somebody without experience using a rope and a very difficult climb with no rope).

When I reached the plateau, I pulled myself up and walked over to the other side to find an easier route down. But there wasn't one. The other routes off the plateau were sheer rock, straight down. The crack where I had left the rope was the easiest way down. The rope, as I had already determined, was useless because it didn't reach the floor.

I climbed off the plateau and back down into the crack to where the rope was wedged. I left it there, and proceeded down. The climb was over. I just needed to make it down. I took it slowly, felt my way, and reached the bottom safely.

Once I became an experienced climber and shed "Muscle-Head Matt" for good, I established a cardinal rule: never free solo anything that I had already done with a rope. I broke that rule only once.

It happened on a route I had done a bunch of times with a rope. Each time I was up there, I kept thinking it would be a perfect solo route. It was 800 feet, 5 pitches. (Pitch is climber-speak for length; a pitch is 165 feet of rope.) It started out as a 5.8- or 5.9-rated climb. But in order to not repeat myself, I decided to do a 5.10 variation.

The variation was cool. I climbed up the first 150 feet of a thin finger crack and felt confident that I would be fine free soloing the route. I passed two climbers who were on ropes. It's kind of freaky for a climber who is roped up to watch somebody without a rope climb by them.

After I carefully passed the climbers, I reached the tricky part. There was a bulge right at a crack that required two hand jams followed by an unorthodox friction move. I climbed the bulge and executed the move. I stayed in control, but as soon as I stood up, my foot was just inches from popping out.

My heart started racing. I held fast and thought, *Slow down your heart.* My next thought was that it would've been awful if those climbers I passed had to watch me plummet past them.

There was still one bigger bulge above me that I had to climb. At that point, I was questioning my commitment. I had broken my rule not to free solo something I had roped. I made that rule because it kept me focused and in control. But I went ahead and did it.

I reached the next bulge. My heart was beating in triple time, and I kept trying to slow it down. There was too much dangerous exposure on the route, because at that point I was seven hundred feet off the deck of the steep, sloping face where the ledges were.

Though I made it without incident, that was the last time I broke my cardinal rule.

Any responsible climber on a new route should always be thinking, *Can I downclimb this route?* As you go up, you must focus on every move. However, you also have to work in both directions because there may come a point in a route, even as far as a thousand feet up, where you determine that you can't continue and need to downclimb the route. When that happens, you set aside ego for safety. No matter how well you know the rock, you have to know yourself better.

Climbing was an important phase of my education about nature. It was something I immensely enjoyed. Being on the rock was blissful. It was one of the few things I found that completely emptied my head of all thoughts and distractions. All of my attention had to be focused on one thing.

At that point in my life, I didn't know how to meditate. Climbing took the place of that. It channeled my head to a point that forced me to relax and surrender to nature.

If a climber doesn't surrender to the rock, he is not going to climb well. When someone watches an accomplished climber, they marvel at the way their back muscles ripple and their legs and arms attach to the rock. Most people think, *That person must be in amazing physical shape and have strong hands.* That's all true, but that is not even the half of it.

For a climber, it is about letting go of those thoughts. The climber cannot think about the physicality, because there is so much technique involved in the way you must balance your feet and your hands to take pressure off them. The climber must take a soft approach, rather than an aggressive one, or he will not be a climber for long.

When I first started climbing, fear was pervasive. I was scared of heights and had thoughts of falling. But once I learned to move over the rock the way nature wanted me to move over it, I felt like I was doing the right thing. Although I was free soloing routes two thousand feet up, those climbs weren't a death wish. I wasn't doing anything that was out of place to the degree that it sparked an uncontrollable fear. I was doing what I was supposed to be doing.

Chapter Five

THE ANCIENT FOOT MESSENGERS

From the age of six, running was my pathway to feeling free and the vehicle for my exploration of the land. My father would take me out jogging with him. I loved when he would vary our route so I could see different things. Even at that age, I realized that running was a way to put a smile on my face and to explore my surroundings.

Throughout high school, I was an avid runner. I could run a fifty-two-second quarter mile at a time when adults were winning gold in the Olympics with a forty-nine. But I wanted to run across the plains and up mountains to see life, not around a track. I didn't want to run for fitness; I wanted to run for awareness, as my forebearers had.

When I moved to the Sierras at age seventeen, I ran every day. I started out going on short runs of six miles or so. I then worked my way to running up Half Dome, which was twenty miles round-trip. But during that time, running remained a social pursuit. It was somehow ingrained in me that twenty-six miles—the distance of a marathon— was the farthest you were supposed to run. But as I began to study running and what it meant to the lifestyle I was choosing, that would all change.

At the time I became interested in running, America was in the middle of a jogging craze. People were running in greater numbers than at any time in the past. This led to the creation of specialty shoes for running. Recreational runners bought the shoes in droves, and eventually created a multibillion-dollar market.

Nike, then a nascent company, led the charge in creating different styles of running shoes. In my teens, I ran in a Nike shoe called the Air Tierra. The shoe was like a rubber moccasin, with no cushioning in the forefront and just a half inch of padding in the heel. I loved it. You could corner the edges of the rocks and maintain full control.

After I ran the heck out of my Air Tierras, I bought a second pair at a thrift shop and beat those up as well. But when I went to buy another pair, I couldn't find the shoe anywhere. I called Nike and asked why they stopped producing it. The customer service representative told me that too many people were getting stone bruises, so the company discontinued the shoe. The shoe that replaced it was beefed up in the heel and heavily padded in the front.

Soon the market was flooded with similar shoes. I didn't like training in the newer shoes that had come on the market. I remember looking at a pair of gel-filled shoes and thinking, *If I put these big cushions on my feet, I'm just going to destroy my body because my feet will not be able to hit the ground naturally.* That was when I started to experiment with different footwear.

I began running in my kung fu shoes. The thin sole allowed me to feel the impact of the ground. I actually came up with the idea from my martial arts training, which was based on the concept of impact training.

As a martial artist, I did impact training with my hands. I would punch wood constantly to build up cartilage and tissues. I knew from that type of training that the impact actually built strong, healthy joints. I decided to translate that to my feet.

Studies of impact training in martial arts have shown that martial artists who train on boards build cartilage, whereas martial artists who train on cushy, foam bags break down their bodies. The way to keep the body the healthiest is to connect it to the impact. The same principle applies to the feet and legs. You can't have a lot of cushioning and not expect that you are going to deteriorate something—which is the running-shoe myth.

The running-shoe myth, sold to consumers by manufacturers, is that cushioned shoes give a runner bounce and prevent injuries. But we now know from numerous long-term studies that running shoes have likely created more injuries than they have prevented.

Dr. Irene Davis, a sports scientist at the University of Delaware, tested runners in shoes and in bare feet. Her studies showed that when you are wearing a running shoe, your heel hits first, which is called a heel strike. This creates a hard ground-reaction force, or upward vibration, that has an impact on the legs. However, in bare feet, there is less ground-reaction force. The runner lands more on the midfoot and less on the heel, causing a reduced impact on the legs.

Dr. Davis and others have shown that rather than protecting our feet, running shoes actually harm them by causing the foot to overpronate. In normal pronation, the outside part of the heel hits the ground first. The foot then rolls inward at fifteen degrees, causing the weight of the body to be distributed evenly over the foot. When a foot overpronates, the foot rolls farther inward, which throws off the weight distribution. In this situation, the ankle does not properly stabilize the body. Normal pronation occurs best in bare feet.

When running barefoot, the feet receive continuous information from the ground. This allows the runner to respond to changes in what's underfoot much faster. You can use every part to your foot, which prevents overusing any one part and creating adverse shock in the ankle and leg. You can use your toes to cradle a rock for better balance and traction. When you hit the corner of a rock, your foot takes the impact and molds around the rock, whereas in a running shoe, the stiff edge of the shoe can catch the rock and roll your ankle.

Barefoot running was a concept I began to grasp in my teens. After I moved to Yosemite, I often ran barefoot, even in the winter. I found that running barefoot in the snow was good for conditioning. I also found that running barefoot in the snow increased the circulation in my capillaries. My feet never got cold, because I was constantly stimulating my capillaries and increasing the circulation in my feet.

Barefoot running led to my exploration of sandals as a far superior alternative to funkified Nikes. I began experimenting with sandals made of many different materials, including yucca, rawhide, leather, worn-out flip-flops, and old tires. My goal was to find footwear as close to a moccasin as possible so I could maintain a natural running position and be in touch with the ground.

Rawhide sandals are ideal for running. They are made from the hides of large animals such as elk. They work well in colder weather, as I can leave the fur on for a tiny bit of added comfort. I can also use the coarse hair grain to provide added traction in certain types of soil, such as damp clay. Rawhide sandals are stiff at first. It feels like you are running on plastic, but as you break them in, they conform to your feet.

How long a pair of rawhide sandals last depends on the quality of the hide. Provided that the hide is cut from the upper part of the neck, elk can last a maximum of three hundred miles. Buffalo hide, which is thicker, can take you six hundred to seven hundred miles. Tanning the leather slightly can increase the durability. This makes the hide last longer because it forms around the ground as you move and therefore wears more evenly.

Two-Ply Rawhide Sandals
WITH FUR LEFT ON

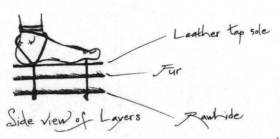

Leather top sole

Fur

Side view of Layers

Rawhide

Leaving the fur on adds more contour to the foot, provides better insulation, takes less time to produce, and the fur does not wear out before the rawhide does.

Yucca Fiber Sandals

FIVE FEET
TWISTED CORDAGE
(6mm)

Twine fiber to
the 5 foot cord

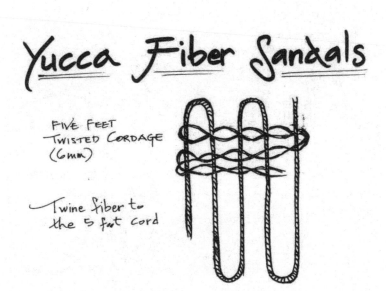

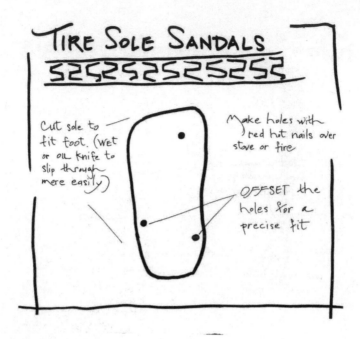

TIRE SOLE SANDALS

Cut sole to fit foot. (Wet or oil knife to slip through mere easily)

Make holes with red hot nails over stove or fire

OFFSET the holes for a precise fit

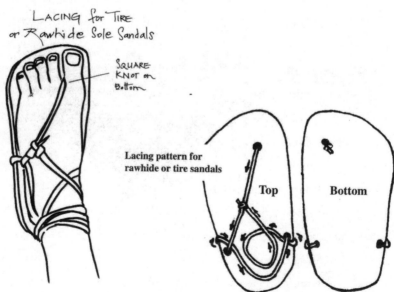

LACING for Tire or Rawhide Sole Sandals

SQUARE KNOT on Bottom

Lacing pattern for rawhide or tire sandals

Top

Bottom

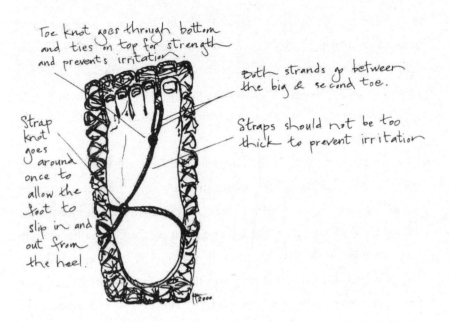

Toe knot goes through bottom and ties on top for strength and prevents irritation.

Both strands go between the big & second toe.

Strap knot goes around once to allow the foot to slip in and out from the heel.

Straps should not be too thick to prevent irritation

Yucca sandals have several advantages. They can be woven anywhere yucca grows, eliminating the need for killing an animal to make the sandals. I found that the Yucca sandals allow my feet to grip the ground closely. If they are woven tightly, the Yucca grabs the soil and rock well, even when the rock is wet. This helps when I'm hunting. With my feet holding firm, I'm able to throw more accurately. They also breathe nicely in both cold and heat. The downside is that they take longer to make and they wear out fast. I can get only about forty-five miles per pair.

Another advantage to sandals is that they are easy to make and that other fibers work just as well as yucca. No matter where I am, if I lose a sandal in a flash flood, I can make another pair in an hour. On some islands, there are different types of bark or cottonwood that will work. Agave plants can also be used—so, as one of my friends joked, if you really know what you are doing, you can have a tequila while making your sandals.

Fiber sandals also work well for tracking. They don't make any sound from step to step, so they are very effective for stalking animals. On the flip side, they are also good if you don't want to be tracked. The fibers break up the pattern left by the sole. These work even better than placing felt on the bottoms of your shoes, which is a standard practice for military avoiding the enemy.

For extreme survival situations, tire sandals are the best because they are the most durable. Three-quarter-inch tire sandals can last up to ten years. They can be made with old belted tires, which are readily available. The sidewalls work best because they are not as stiff. Generally, sidewalls are not lined with steel, and they also have a natural curve and arch support built in. Though the grip on the foot is not as tight and pure as sandals made from yucca or rawhide, the tire material imitates the cartilage in the body. This will make a first-time wearer sore until their cartilage toughens up.

Sandals provide a more natural way of running than $250 midstrike shoes with custom orthotics. After I switched to sandals and established a more natural stride, I didn't suffer from any hip, ankle, or knee injuries.

I also found that running in sandals puts my feet in better touch with the ground. I love the feeling of being closer to the earth rather than plodding along in a pair of funkified Nikes. Scott Jurek, a professional distance runner, once looked at my sandals and commented, "You must feel really connected to the earth running in sandals like that."

Indeed I do.

Even as I explored barefoot running and running in sandals, I still did not have a profound connection to running. My entire relationship with running changed in my late teens. I was in a public library rummaging through the free box of magazines when I stumbled upon an article about the Tarahumara Indians in the May 1976 issue of *National Geographic*. The story focused on their ability to effortlessly run long distances. In a two-day period, the best runners could cover 435 miles, which is equal to sixteen marathons. Even an average Tarahumara could run more than 100 miles without stopping or suffering sore joints.

To this day, the Tarahumara are considered the greatest runners in the world. Running has been part of the Tarahumara culture since the 1500s. It was a means of both athletic expression and survival. They delivered mail and intervillage communications and hunted for food on foot. While the article was inspirational for someone interested in long-distance running, what was most interesting to me was that the Tarahumara ran in handmade sandals rather than shoes.

At the time, I was spending half the money I earned on running shoes. I was also suffering from a variety of running-related injuries such as shin splints, persistent pain in my right knee, and hamstring injuries. I had already begun searching for an alternative.

To become the most efficient runner possible, I needed to see the Tarahumara Indians and study them in action. I was eager to examine the Tarahumara's sandals, as well as to study their running technique and to gain knowledge, inspiration, and wisdom.

When I set out on the trip, I didn't have much information to go on. I knew the Tarahumara lived in Copper Canyon, located in the southwestern part of the Mexican state of Chihuahua, about two hours south of the Arizona border. Copper Canyon is a vast system of six canyons, so I needed to find a starting point. The consensus from what I read was that I should go to a small town called Creel, which I did. When I reached Creel, I hopped off the bus and starting running.

I searched for the Tarahumara on their own terms—on foot. The land was very dry, and the canyon walls were green, like oxidized copper (hence the name). I found small village settlements and met several Indians, but I didn't feel comfortable invading their sacred space. Instead, I spent most of my time watching the men run and observing how they interacted. One thing was true: they were always running. The trails were constantly in use, and I seldom saw the men walking.

I spent ten days running, seeing the land, getting in shape, and orienting myself mentally to the running techniques of the Tarahumara. Watching them was a beautiful sight. It looked like the way a human should run. Their backs were ramrod straight, and they pointed their toes down. This caused them to land midfoot rather than striking with their heel first, which is a result of having the toes up. What was most noticeable was that the looks on their faces showed that they loved to run. There was no grimacing or grunting. They were actually smiling as they traversed the land.

The main thing I learned from them was how to strike the foot on the ground. They recognize that the nerves in the feet are as sensitive as the nerves in the genitals. Treating those nerves kindly proves to be the key to running distances. They also understand that running involves a "mass spring" that transfers potential energy into kinetic energy through the tendons and ligaments.

The tribe showed me how running could be a spiritual part of life. Running to them is like water flowing downhill, feeding the crops as it goes. The images of them running are beautiful. They sew their own clothes out of bright fabrics, and when you see them in the distance, they look like moving flowers dotting the trail.

I also observed their sandals closely. I was somewhat surprised when I realized the sandals were simply hard, heavy chunks of rubber. It was astounding to see how well they could run on something so hard. People think of rubber as soft and bouncy. But these are not wealthy people with resources, so they use very heavy semitruck tires for the soles. Used semi tires are inexpensive, and when made into sandal soles, they last fifteen years, even with the amount of miles the Tarahumara run.

When I finally held one of their sandals, I was even more shocked. The sandals weighed *three pounds* each. I wondered how they ran in them at all. Not only did they feel like leg weights but they were very stiff. Healthwise, the thing the sandals had going for them was that they were hard. They weren't cushions breaking the runners' bodies down like superlight running shoes stuffed with foam and gel.

I had brought my leather huaraches on the trip, which were the type of sandals the Tarahumara made before they used tires. My footwear intrigued the Indians I met. Many of them made comments about how fast I could run in light shoes made of leather. On a future visit when I showed up in thin tire sandals, I was amused to find the Indians were slightly jealous. They requested that I bring them some thin tires when I next visited.

It wasn't surprising to hear the positive health effects that so much running had on the Tarahumara. The Tarahumara were practically immortal compared to Americans. In addition to the miles covered, the Tarahumara's diet also contributed to their overall health. Diabetes and heart disease were virtually nonexistent.

Many articles have been written about tesguino, the corn beer that the Tarahumara consume at festivals. It was also detailed in the book *Born to Run*, by Christopher McDougall, which talked about the bacchanalian-style feasts they had the night before long runs. The truth is, they don't have those festivals very often. Americans like to think about drunken Indians, but they don't drink beer and rarely drink fermented corn.

I found that they drink more tea than anything. Whenever I stopped in a village, they always had a pot of pinole, which is hot tea made with pine needles. They keep it over a fire in big clay pots. They are such a corn-based culture that sometimes on top of the pinole tea they serve corn tortillas. They live and breathe corn, especially the poorer people, because they can't afford to grow or buy most other foods.

The traditional, Western view is that the corn eaten by the Tarahumara is stored as glycogen and then converted to energy. This serves as the explanation why the Tarahumara have such endurance on long runs.

Nutritionists teach us to do calculations where you burn x amount of energy and then replace that with y amount of calories. Under this scenario, in a 26.2-mile marathon, an average runner will burn about 2,600 calories. Following this logic, if a Tarahumara were to run 435 miles in two days, he would burn 43,500 calories.

But that's an American concept that really doesn't hold validity in ancient and Native American cultures. It also doesn't make sense that someone can store up or consume 43,500 calories in a few days. In fact, what happens in traditional cultures is that the runners burn so many calories and replace them with so few that over time their metabolisms become increasingly more efficient.

Take a Native American tribe such as the Navajo, whom I have seen up close. If they ate the same amount of calories as we do in our normal lives, they would gain fifteen pounds in a month. It wouldn't be entirely their fault they got fat. Genetically, they would still have the same superefficient metabolism. In our Western and European culture, we have entered a phase where our metabolisms are much more rapid because we haven't been in starvation mode the way traditional people have been.

The same is true in Kenya. There is an abundance of great distance runners from Kenya, all of whom are rail thin and do not consume an abundance of calories. This is because they have lowered their metabolism to the point where they don't require the same number of calories as an average American for energy.

Seeing how effective this was in Native American cultures, I went on a lifelong pursuit to make my body more efficient as a runner and use fewer calories. After a few weeks of going into starvation mode, I found that I needed half the calories to function at the same level. Of course, as soon as you return to three hearty meals a day, you've blown all that. You have to maintain yourself at close to the same level.

Obviously, we don't have the genetic predisposition to go as far as a Native American, but we do have the ability to readjust our metabolisms for short periods of time in training. I sought to find a balance that would allow me to live for long periods of time in the wild.

I knew that running had been central to the lifestyle of early hunter-gatherers. They ran to hunt food. They ran to avoid being attacked by animals. They ran to move from place to place quickly. And likely, the men ran to impress the ladies. I knew that to live in the wilderness and be able to hunt effectively I would need to understand running and be able to explain it to others.

The transition to natural running requires special training that should be undertaken in stages. You can't just take off your running shoes, hit the trail in bare feet or sandals, and expect to feel anything but pain. You don't want to race—pun intended—into anything full-on, or you will get injured.

To run in bare feet or sandals requires an understanding of the larger picture of running and a concept of what keeps the body strong. If a runner has worn cushioned shoes for most his life, he will have a weak body. Cushioned shoes compromise the body. His cartilage and his joints through his knees and hips will be weak. For somebody who has used that kind of compromising support, if they put on hard rubber sandals and think their body will feel better, they are in for a world of hurt.

Any transition to sandals must be undertaken gradually. You must first strengthen the feet before moving to sandals. The first step in the transition is to go barefoot as much as you can without hurting yourself. The best way is to start out walking in bare feet and then slowly build up to running. After walking around barefoot as much as possible for a week, try running a half mile.

Depending on where you live, you can try running barefoot on different surfaces. The best surfaces are grass, dirt, or sand. However, someone who lives in a big city should run on pavement once in a while. The idea is to have that feeling where your toes are grabbing the ground. Reaching that feeling will strengthen the underside of your feet and cause you to land more softly.

Over time, barefoot running will build a quarter inch of cartilage on the bottom of the feet. At that point, when you run on pavement, you will not feel that pounding slap of the feet. Once you have that feeling, you can start experimenting with traditional, thinner-soled sandals designed for rougher terrains.

I can run barefoot on any landscape with the exception of extremely hot sand. But it is a matter of the pace and how much I want to be able to look around and observe without worrying about what's on the ground. Sometimes going barefoot in rough terrain causes me to miss everything around me, because I'm looking down at my feet the entire time. When I run on new land, I wear sandals so I can observe.

In addition to strengthening the underside feet muscles, barefoot running adds more spring to the step and ultimately provides for a softer landing. Running on harder soles, such as rawhide or tire sandals, also builds up cartilage. A runner who wants to maintain a healthy body needs a balance of all those elements. The Tarahumara, for instance, know how important barefoot running is, so they occasionally take off their sandals and run barefoot just to keep their bodies healthy.

I do half my runs barefoot and half in thin-soled sandals. The exception is wintertime. When it is really cold, I will now wear a low-cut, barefoot-style running shoe with a tiny bit of padding. If I did that all the time, it would start to weaken my body. But because I do it sparingly, it doesn't.

Ultimately, a transition to natural running will prevent joint pain. Consider the Tarahumara and natural distance runners from African countries. When they are old men, they are still running constantly. They don't experience joint problems. This is not because they have über-genetics. It is simply because from the time they were young, they put their bodies on a different track from Western runners and did not attempt to overprotect their limbs with cushions on their feet.

Instead of running in natural shoes and surroundings, can you use a StairMaster, treadmill, or elliptical machine? Sure. It's not the best solution, but sometimes it may be the only one if you want to exercise. Inherently, anytime we go against the grain of nature and use technology, it will compromise something in our health and well-being. However, sometimes you have to use technology because of the circumstances.

Of course, it would be far better for the body to hike up a trail. You are outside, breathing fresh air. You also receive the benefits of walking down the trail, which creates a different neuromuscular sensation.

Running teaches you to have spring. The body is taking in the force, rather than pushing out of it. Bikers who never run are terrible runners. Despite the fact that they have muscular legs, they don't know how to take in impact; they only know how to push out. When they run it is awkward, because they have the strength to push, but they don't have the strength to land.

The ability to be able to run fluidly is a constant thought process that eventually becomes a natural one. Running starts with a conscious awareness of how you walk and move throughout the day, not just when you put on your running shoes. Most people don't even think about the way they walk. They just put one foot in front of another, and that is the same feeling they should try and achieve when they run.

I love to run for two reasons. The first is that it allows me to see new terrain. The other is that it feels good to be moving.

When I looked at the Tarahumara men running down a cliff side, they always had big smiles on their faces. Kids are the same way. When they have that spontaneous thought to run down a sand dune, it puts a smile on their face. You can take huge strides, and because it's soft, you won't hurt yourself if you face-plant. Happiness is a large part of running.

With the knowledge I had gathered from observing the Tarahumara and my experimentation with barefoot running and with sandals, I began to focus on running lightly, easily, and smoothly, all while searching for a harmony with the land. One Native American I met summed up the perfect feeling of running. He said: "When you run, you never run over the earth. What happens is that the earth just starts moving under you, and you move your legs with it."

That is the ultimate feeling of running, as you no longer feel like you are running. It is the point you reach when you feel like running is something you are supposed to be doing, not any sort of physical struggle. If you want to run all day, that is a great place to set your mind. It prevents you from using excess energy and allows the earth to dictate your movements. You feel like the earth is pushing you along as it rotates under you, and rather than exerting energy, you must figure out how to dance as varying terrain and obstacles come at you.

Confirmation that I had achieved that feeling came later, on my second visit to the Tarahumara. In addition to what I had learned, one of the most satisfying aspects of my time with the tribe was that I made a lasting connection. They branded me "Rara Miri El Blonco," which translates to "the White Tarahumara" or "white foot runner." I wear that as a badge of honor.

Chapter Six

PREPARING FOR AN EXTREME RUN

E veryone talks about finding his or her identity. For most people, there are experiences that become the building blocks of this process. These experiences begin to add up, and the sum total of them becomes the person's identity. Whether consciously or unconsciously, everyone goes through the process in some form or another.

When I turned nineteen, I was just like any other human trying to separate myself from other humans. I was working in a mountaineering shop in Mammoth Lakes, California. Though I performed the tasks to the best of my abilities, it was still just a job. My real focus was working to perfect my climbing and becoming a better distance runner. I felt that by somehow combining climbing and running and using those to explore the land, I could end my lateral drift and establish my own unique identity.

One day, I happened upon a book titled *The Pacific Crest Trail, Volume 1: California*. As the book detailed, the Pacific Crest Trail stretches 2,638 miles from the Mexico/California border to the Washington/Canada border. The California section, by far the longest section at some 1,700 miles, covers the length of the state. Therein lies its majesty.

The trail passes through every climate and nature zone the United States has to offer. As its name states, it runs along the crest of some of the most stunning mountains in the world. It climbs at points to fourteen thousand feet, dips down into the hottest, driest desert, and crosses rivers, towns, and even our busiest highways.

The book's focus was on hiking the Pacific Crest Trail. In the beginning, it talked about allowing five to six months to complete the trail. It mentioned that a couple named Ray and Jenny Jardine completed the journey in three months and three weeks. Another man, Bob Holtel, ran the trail in 110 days at the pace of a marathon a day, though he rested 46 additional days, meaning that he averaged about 16.5 miles a day. With my training, I was pretty sure I could blow those times away.

I had first heard about the Pacific Crest Trail when I was eighteen. Several of my climbing friends talked about hiking the trail, but running the trail seemed like an elusive dream. Even though the guidebooks said it took several months to complete, we were all certain we could do it faster. But no one actually tried.

I had friends who were in great shape and were accomplished runners. One of my friends, Bruce Davis, used to tell a story about running out into the wild for a day, spending the night, and running back the next day. He had worn a fanny pack and carried a bivy sack and a change of clothes. He was elated by the experience, and I could see by the light in his eyes that something had hit him really hard. It was a simple way to connect with the backcountry carrying minimal gear.

Ideas for long runs circulated in my head for years. I considered entering the Western States 100-Mile race. I contemplated running the John Muir Trail, which stretches 211 miles through the Sierra Nevada mountains. The dilemma was whether I wanted to start entering long races or to keep to the purity of running by going out and finding my own backcountry trails.

The more I read *The Pacific Crest Trail* and the more I thought about running the PCT, the stronger the pull became. It was a pursuit that would help define me, as well as teach me things about the land that I couldn't learn on long day runs. Rather than entering competitive races, I decided that running for the sake of exploration was the route I would take.

At first glance, running 1,700 miles might seem impossible. But from my research I was learning that running great distances was actually more natural for humans than most people realize. Several scientists who undertook lengthy studies concluded that humans are actually built to run extreme distances.

In one study, the noted anthropologists Daniel Lieberman of Harvard University and Campbell Rolian of the University of Calgary determined that short toes make humans better suited to running than to walking. They tested fifteen people both running and walking on a pressure-sensitive treadmill. They discovered that an increased toe length of just 20 percent doubled the amount of energy required to run and produced additional shock on the foot.

Their conclusion was human bodies are ideally equipped to run long distances.

In doing so, we are using our bodies the way our hominid forebearers did millions of years ago. In what is known as the "endurance running hypothesis," scientists and anthropologists believe that running for extended lengths of time is an adapted trait. The evidence suggests that it was the catalyst that forced *Homo erectus* to evolve from its apelike ancestors because they needed to obtain food.

For me, such information only fed my desire to take a run few had taken before, and it suggested that not only would my body hold up but it was actually built for the journey.

When I broke the news to friends that I was going to run the Pacific Crest Trail, nearly everyone I told was supportive and offered encouragement. However, several ultra-distance runners discouraged me, which came as a surprise. I expected more support from people who ran more than I did. I wasn't bragging that I was setting out to break the record. I explained that I was just planning to run the trail and see what happened. Despite knowing how physically fit I was, they were skeptical that my body would hold up.

At that time, the prevailing wisdom among ultra-distance runners was that they didn't peak until age thirty. Runners who regularly won races were closer to forty. The reason for this was mostly pacing and tactical smarts. It wasn't that younger runners weren't capable of winning those races; rather it was just that they would start too hard and not know how to pace themselves over fifty or a hundred miles.

I was fairly certain that my body would hold up. I was running like a madman. It was wintertime. I would wake up in the morning and run twenty miles before 10 a.m.—my morning jog in the snow. My weeks were filled with one hundred and fifty total miles over varying terrain. There were times I pushed myself extra-hard for consecutive days. I would run sixty-five miles one day, fifty the next, and maybe forty the third day. But I had never run those distances consecutively for weeks. I had little concept of how many miles I could do for days on end.

I did have other advantages. At that point in my life, I had never owned a car. I was always on my feet. I didn't even have a bicycle. I made a concerted effort to stay off wheels of any kind. My primary mode of transportation was on foot, which allowed me to stay connected with the earth every step of the day.

The thought of running the PCT brought on a rush of tremendous joy. Not only was it a historic trail, it was a journey that represented freedom in all regards. As much as I loved running across the land, those runs required brainpower. The beauty about getting on a trail is that you don't have to think. You hop on the trail and put one foot in front of the other. The next day, you do the same thing. There is a meditative feeling to being on a trail versus running cross-country.

It was a perfect time to run the PCT. The trail had just been officially completed. Previously, there were sections where people had to improvise the route because the trail was not continuous. Depending on the route taken, there were shortcuts in the uncompleted areas, particularly in one twelve-mile section that had not been finished because it was overgrown with brush and trees.

In May 1996, I felt I was ready. I headed to Seal Beach in Southern California to stay with family. The city was close to the Mexican border where I would start. I had done a lot of mountain training, so I reasoned that a couple weeks of flat training would be beneficial. I also began putting together the supplies I would need. Some supplies—very few, actually—I would carry rolled up in a cloth and tied around my waist. Others I would ship to post office drops along the trail.

I was trying to capture the feeling of what it means to take off running with only the essential gear I needed tied around my waist. To me that offered the ultimate freedom. It showed that I had developed my skills to the point where I was confident I didn't need a backpack and could travel a great distance with only the absolute essentials.

I had only about four hundred dollars to my name, so I decided to ask energy bar companies for products in exchange for publicity. I called PowerBar and Clif Bar. PowerBar sent me a hundred bars. Clif Bar was a little less generous. They first offered me a wholesale price. Then they ended up sending me sixty bars complimentary. I understood their reluctance because nobody knew who I was. I was just some kid saying he was going to run the state of California.

At that point, I thought that once I finished the trail and broke the record, they would all be calling me with endorsement offers. I wasn't convinced I would accept them, but the prospect of the offers was somewhat motivating.

I also stocked up on sunflower seeds and chia seeds. I had learned about the power of chia seeds from my research on Native Americans. Legend had it that when Geronimo was on the warpath and nearly starving, chia seeds sustained him. Many native tribes throughout the Southwest claimed that chia was the superfood of the land and that you could go hundreds of miles on just a few teaspoons of the seed, often referred to as the "food of the gods." At the time, chia cost only about ninety-nine cents a pound—though once it became a fad, the price spiked to thirty-two dollars a pound.

I boxed up supplies to be shipped to the mail drops I chose from the PCT book. For the California section of the PCT, the book listed eighteen drops that were on the trail itself, rather than in nearby towns. I could have done the trail without any drops by purchasing food in the towns the trail runs through, but using drops would allow me to have the foods I wanted rather than relying on what was available. I also didn't want to be forced to detour for supplies. I ended up choosing five drops based on the terrain in the area and what I thought my needs would be.

I planned to travel light. The fact that I was running and not hiking forced the issue even further. I took a five-by-five-foot piece of cloth that would serve as a blanket and laid it out on the ground. I placed my bivy sack, my water filter, my maps, extra shorts, and sandals, as well as my food, on the cloth and then rolled it up. I tied it around my waist. I slung a water bladder over my shoulder. Everything I carried had to serve a purpose.

I had very little margin for error.

Chapter Seven

RUNNING CALIFORNIA

June 1, 1996, was a hot, dry day on the California-Mexico border. The ground was singed from lack of rain and looked like a rippled potato chip. I was wearing shorts and regular running shoes to protect my feet. My cloth lined with supplies was tied around my waist. When I arrived in the small town of Campo, I walked south about a mile into the middle of the desert until I reached a barbed wire fence.

Staked in the ground next to the fence was a sign that read "Mexico" with an arrow pointing south. Another sign pointing north to a trailhead read "Pacific Crest Trail." I signed my name on the PCT register that was inside a small metal box. I then turned north toward the trail that was faintly carved out of the brush, and I started running.

There was no adrenaline burst when I started. I had a sense of bliss that I was about to see new grounds and that I was making the journey unencumbered. I felt like I had been to one of those spiritual retreats where everyone gives up their possessions.

I began thinking ahead. I knew there would be no water for at least twenty miles. Any groundwater in the area that came down the mountains from the winter snow would have long since dried up. I immediately focused on conserving water.

The first day was harder than I expected. It was so hot and humid that my feet began swelling almost immediately. After just one day, it was clear that traditional shoes weren't going to work. That night, I turned my running shoes into sandals. I cut the toe box out of the shoes and removed the tongue, giving my feet space to move around and spread out properly when they hit ground.

On the second day, I came upon two men who were hiking down the trail I was running up. Judging by all the gear they were carrying, they were day-trippers. They were moving at a good clip. As I approached, I greeted them with a wave.

"Wetbacks!" one of them said, pointing up the trail. "There's some wetbacks up there!"

I stopped. "Are they dangerous?" I asked in a concerned tone.

"I mean, I don't think so," the other said. "But they're Mexicans."

I cracked a smile.

"Be careful," the first guy said.

"Will do," I said, giving them a salute.

I continued up the hill. Sure enough, when I came around over the top of the hill, I spotted five guys hiking through the brush. They were wearing beaten-up blue jeans, dirty white T-shirts, and monstrous smiles. Clearly, they were happy to be in California starting their new lives. They all waved at me, and I waved back.

I was surprised by how much I was struggling in the first few days. The heat was affecting me, and my body hadn't adjusted to the task at hand. On the first day, despite being fresh, I covered only twenty miles. I was disappointed that my body wasn't responding better.

To improve blood flow, in the first few nights, I found a spot on a slight slope and lay with my head downhill and my feet uphill. I crawled into my bivy sack and put the piece of cloth I had brought over my body. This covered my body while exposing my legs to air. Keeping my legs uphill kept the blood out of them. I felt that this recovered them faster and left me feeling fresher the next morning. I ended up repeating this sleeping process every night of the trip.

Over the next few days, I covered roughly twenty-seven miles a day. For me, that was not much. I kept thinking, *This isn't right. I've run sixty-five miles in a day. Why can't I produce more? Is my body failing me?*

Water was at a premium early on, as I knew it would be. In addition to the year being unusually dry, it was summertime, with highs reaching one hundred degrees. Most hikers attempting the entire PCT start out in the spring because the land is still moist from the winter snow. Many of the springs and water sources mentioned in guidebooks were dried up. There were several days when I wouldn't find any water the entire day.

But even in a dehydrated state, with each passing day I seemed to become more a part of the land. I stopped feeling like a runner or a hiker, and I started to feel like I belonged. I started to feel like the land was moving under me, rather than me pushing over it. Achieving that feeling allowed me to increase my daily distance without any pushback from my body, and I hoped to establish a rhythm.

I zipped through the Laguna Mountains. Once the elevation increased, the shady oaks kept the sun off me. As I came down into the Anza-Borrego Desert, the climate shifted dramatically. The contrast was jarring. I was fully exposed to the sun, and it was torturously hot and dry.

One evening at sunset, I stopped to sleep for the night. I was out of water and feeling dry-mouthed. I reasoned that if I slept, then I would be starting up again in the hot sun, not knowing where I would be able to fill my water bladder. Despite the fact that I was tired, I decided to continue running through the night until I found water.

This was the type of decision I often had to make in survival situations. I had to ignore my immediate needs and look ahead. Sleep was important but water was more critical.

It turned out to be the right choice. The terrain was very open and there were no snakes, which would have made night running dangerous. The night sky was so clear that the trail was illuminated by a three-quarter moon that lit my way over the open terrain.

Early the next morning I found water. I pressed on across the desert. Soon, I rose into the San Jacinto Mountains. For most of the way, chaparral, a wiry shrubbery, brushed at my legs and arms. The climb was nothing compared to the descent. Leaving San Jacinto, the plunge was some eight thousand feet, passing through nearly every life zone in the state.

The down run was intense. The trail was steep with switchbacks. The drop was greater than hiking from the top to the bottom of the Grand Canyon—twice. The previous year I had trained in the Grand Canyon, so I was used to hitting the four-thousand-feet elevation mark and being done. But this time when I hit it, there was yet another Grand Canyon to go.

I made it down in about three hours, but I was completely out of food. I hadn't started out with a lot of food, to keep the weight of my pack down. I had finished all my food except for a tiny bit of chia seeds. Those would have to sustain me for several days until I picked up my first shipment or reached a town.

The San Jacinto Mountains were twenty miles from the top to the bottom. As depleted as I was, I still had to cross the desert flats and then run back up the other side to reach the town of Big Bear, which is basically at the same elevation. In Big Bear, I could find food.

I gutted out the ten miles across the desert, passing underneath the

I-10 freeway, and then began the climb to Big Bear. I could feel my blood sugar crashing. I was having a hard time even lifting my arms to keep them in sync with my legs. However, my legs were in such good shape that I was able to run without pumping my arms. I let my arms dangle at my sides like an ape and continued running.

A couple miles before I reached Big Bear, about six thousand feet up, I spotted a car. I was so depleted that at first I thought it was a mirage. But as I drew closer, I could see the outlines of a person hunching over the trunk. This was the first person I had seen since the Mexican immigrants several days earlier.

It was a lady organizing her belongings. I stopped and told her what I was doing. She didn't seem impressed or unimpressed. Actually, I wasn't sure she believed me. I asked if she had any chips or other food that could help me balance my blood sugar. She dug into her pocket and produced some hard candy, for which I was grateful.

When I reached Big Bear, I was happy to see civilization and food. I decided to treat myself—and also to put some much-needed calories in my body. I had twenty dollars on me. My first drop was in Agua Dulce, another 110 miles away. I had shipped both money and supplies, so I wasn't worried about spending money. I went into a diner and downed a burger and a milk shake.

After my all-American dinner, I camped outside of Big Bear. Because of the elevation, the night was bitter cold. When I lay down to go to sleep, my legs were cold. As uncomfortable as I was, my thoughts turned positive. The cold would heal my aching legs. It was the first time during my run that I was fully and willingly surrendering to the elements.

The next morning, I got up at 6 a.m. to get moving. I dropped into the Deep Creek Hot Springs canyon and headed toward the Mojave Desert. I was running down the trail when I came upon a guy sitting in his camp. He looked like he had just woken up. The guy was very fit, unlike some of the hikers I had seen in town.

He had reams of expensive gear strewn out all over the place. There must have been forty pounds of everything from tents and sleeping bags to cooking equipment and hiking boots. It looked like he had bought out the REI store.

Because he was almost directly in my path, I stopped. The guy gestured at the gear. "I bought all this fuckin' gear to hike the trail," he said. "I have a zero-degree sleeping bag, and I was cold last night."

"Really," I said, trying to sound sympathetic.

He shook his head in disgust. "I was going to do the whole trail, but this gear isn't working out for me," he said. "I'm done. If your car is around here, I'd like to get a ride out of here if it's not a problem."

"I'm heading north up the PCT to the border," I said. "I'm on foot."

A perplexed look came across his face. He pointed to my wrap. "With just that?" he said.

I nodded. He was speechless. He didn't know if I was messing with him or if I was some kind of badass. He went back to shuffling his gear, and I went on my way.

As I ran, I thought about people who try to re-create creature comforts in the wild with expensive camping gear. I didn't want to be judgmental. It is better than sitting at home and not trying to enjoy the wilderness. But the true experience of hiking the PCT or camping out in the mountains requires a modicum of separation from your living room.

I couldn't help but see the irony. Ultra-light sleeping bags weighed less than a pound. I had wanted to purchase one for my trip, but they were $250, well above what I could spend. Here was a guy who had an even more expensive zero-degree sleeping bag, and he was cold. In contrast, my system was to use the cold to regenerate my legs.

I smiled. While this guy was anchored to his gear, which would take him an hour to pack up, I had slept better and packed in thirty seconds. I had lived with the land, and it had taken care of me.

Emotionally, it was very Zen-like to wake up every day and know that I had one task: to run north. Most of the trail was two feet wide, with sand, pebbles, mud, or pine needles underfoot, and an endless sky in front of me. Every single step I took, every breath I drew, there was something captivating to behold—from plants and trees to creatures of all shapes, sizes, and sounds. I felt a duality with my body and spirit, as if they were working in unison while my feet danced over the trail.

Not knowing what was over the next hill or around the next curve was exciting. With each amazing vista I took in, I was compelled to push forward to see if there was an even more amazing one over the next hill. Being constantly surprised by the beauty of the terrain was the greatest joy of the journey.

There were obstacles in different parts. As I was coming down out of the San Bernardino Mountains into the Mojave Desert, ticks blanketed me. I had to stop every hundred yards and brush swarms of ticks off my legs. Then I'd run another hundred yards and repeat the process.

I did this for several miles through the area near Silverwood Lake until I reached the desert. Luckily, only a few bit me—on my testicles. That's where they end up when you can't find them. The problem is that you don't notice when they bite you, but when you find them and pull them off, the spot is tender for a couple days.

The Mojave Desert had one bizarre spot. I was running along and hadn't seen anything for eighty miles. Then all of a sudden, the trail crossed a highway right next to a convenience store. It was literally in the middle of nowhere.

I went inside. The store was empty, except for the cashier. I picked out an orange juice and a large bean burrito. I walked up to the counter to pay. The cashier quipped, "Don't eat much, do you?"

I thought he was making fun of me for buying the overstuffed burrito. Preparing to explain to him that I was running the entire PCT, I asked him what he meant. He told me that two hikers who had come in the previous day bought ten Big Ed's ice cream sandwiches (which are as big as they sound), sat down in front of the store, and polished them all off. I thanked him and headed out.

I began to think about the odd human interactions I was having. The people I encountered seemed to be using the trail for their own ends. The Mexican immigrants were using it to escape and rebirth themselves. The day hikers were trying to escape their daily lives. The guy with all the gear didn't seem to be trying to escape anything. But I seemed to be using the trail to find something.

After covering roughly 450 miles using only the supplies I had brought—plus the burger and shake, and burrito and orange juice—I arrived in the town of Agua Dulce to pick up my first drop. Unfortunately, the box was not there. I had mailed the first two boxes the day before I left. I then planned to call my mom at certain intervals so she could mail the other two boxes.

I calculated that I was several days ahead of schedule. I was totally famished, and it was a hundred miles until my next drop in Tehachapi. I had just $1.10 on me. I needed to figure out how to get the most nutrition out of my very limited budget. I ended up buying a bag of corn tortillas, three rotten bananas for half price, and a few limes. That was all I ate for the next hundred miles.

The naturalist John Muir called the High Sierras the "Range of Light." The range has some of the most majestic scenery in the world. There are piney forests interspersed with haphazard grassy meadows. Lakes connected by small fords dot the landscape. Immense conical peaks of granite that reach thirteen thousand feet in parts wall in the entire two-hundred-mile stretch. Even in the summer, the higher elevations are coated with snow and ice. Other sections have glaciers that never fully melt.

Kennedy Meadows is regarded as the gateway to the High Sierras. The area, at an elevation of 6,100 feet, has a small resort, several camp-grounds, and a resupply station for hikers heading up into the High Sierras.

I had shipped my third drop to Kennedy Meadows. Inside was my sleeping bag, a necessity in the High Sierras, as the temperature would drop to the freezing mark. Fortunately, the box was there. I unpacked my coat, the food, and some money. I rerolled my wrap and set back out as fast as I could.

I didn't like stopping for too long in the towns and talking to people. I wanted my interactions to be with the land and its natural elements. Almost on cue, I spotted my first mountain lion.

I was near Walker Pass heading up into the Sierras. The trail I was running on was an open ridge. Immediately adjacent was a ridge where the mountain lion was walking parallel to me.

I slowed down. I wasn't afraid, but I also wasn't sure what the lion would do. The lion kept moving and periodically looked over its shoulder at me. We were paralleling for about a mile. I hoped the mountain lion didn't regard me as an invader of his land, but rather as someone who wanted to learn about it. After a mile, the lion rolled his head at me and split off in a different direction.

In the nearly hundred miles from Kennedy Meadows to Trail Pass, the elevation rises from 6,100 to 11,000 feet. With every thousand feet, the temperature dips a few degrees. I soon realized that the north sides of the peaks had snow and ice in the mornings, while the south sides were slushy because the sun was baking them. I was hitting the north peaks in the morning and the south peaks late in the day. Ideally, I wanted this to be the other way around so that the north peaks would be slushy, allowing me to make my way down. Early in the morning, the north peaks were still frozen solid, leaving me to figure out a way to descend safely.

Depending on the ice and the steepness, I used a host of techniques. I sharpened sticks or used sharp rocks to chisel my way down. Occasionally, I would take sticks and wedge them in the ice below me and slide down. Other times, I would use longer sticks as brakes. I knew that if I started to slide without a braking mechanism I would end up pinballing off the trees.

For a two-hundred-mile stretch, from Mount Whitney to Tuolumne Meadows, the terrain was composed of undulating passes of thirteen thousand feet that quickly dipped to eight thousand feet in a valley and then rose back up to thirteen thousand feet.

The highest point on the PCT is Forester Pass. Officially, the elevation is 13,160, though the sign marks it at 13,200. The most surprising thing about being that high on almost all rocky terrain was the amount and variety of flowers.

Like a driver on a road trip marking towns as destinations, I set out to sleep on the top of every mountain. I had slept on mountain peaks many times before the PCT run. To avoid any nighttime drama, I always found an isolated peak so the bears didn't pay me an unexpected visit in their search for a midnight snack.

Most days, I went to sleep when darkness took hold and woke up just after first light. Some nights provided a welcome deep sleep. Others were too magical to miss.

Before reaching the High Sierras, I had camped on the very top of Mount Baldy at ten thousand feet. The city lights of the Los Angeles Basin glowed in the distance below as far as the eye could see. I knew the hustle and bustle of life was occurring. I could see it, but I was at such a distance that I didn't feel it.

In contrast, the volcanic peaks of the Sierras were lit only by the moonlight. There were no signs of any people. Within a matter of a hundred miles, ten million people had vanished.

In *Zen and the Art of Motorcycle Maintenance*, Robert Pirsig talks about how it is better to travel than to arrive. That is exactly how I felt when I hit the final stretch of the PCT in the Cascade Range. Unlike the Sierras, the Cascades were mostly flat with gently undulating terrain that was a pleasure to run. My legs felt like wheels gently rolling across the land.

The most beautiful area was the Lassen Volcanic National Park. The trail takes you to the east side of Lassen Peak, away from the tourist area located on the west side. Lassen Peak is still an active volcano. The heat from the ground warms the azure geothermal lakes that dominate the area. I swam in one lake that must have been eighty degrees.

The day I arrived in Seiad Valley, the final stopping point before the Oregon border, I ran fifty-five miles through a forest of Douglas fir. It was one of my most productive days in terms of distance. I had found my rhythm. I camped overnight and then went for pancakes in the small town the next morning.

I had heard there was a pancake restaurant that had a standing hikers' challenge: if you could eat three pancakes, your order was on the house. I was hungry and running low on money, so I decided to give it a try. When I entered the restaurant, I immediately spotted the cook. He was a huge man, bearing at least 450 pounds. He had his back turned to me. As he was tending to the pancakes, he shifted to the left, exposing a sign on the wall that read: "Never Trust a Skinny Cook."

"Sir, can I have three pancakes, please?" I asked.

The cook looked me up and down. A slim and fit 160 pounds when I set out, I was now about 145. "Why don't you start with one," he suggested.

And so I had my second sit-down meal of the journey. The pancake was bigger than the plate and three inches thick. I sat down and went to work. I managed to eat the entire pancake, which tasted more like birthday cake. Frankly, it was horrible. I felt so sick that I gave up the challenge. I paid $1.50 and left.

That night, I camped out and reminisced on what I had accomplished. I had been running for fifty-seven days. But my journey really was a series of moments, all different in length, strung together, and I had been present in every moment. My goal had been to finish the trail in a reasonable amount of time. I was curious about by how much I could beat the previous records, not for publicity but for myself. I had proven that a younger person could set an ultra-ultra-distance record and hold up physically. By any measure, I had bettered the fastest time by half.

I probably had the chance to create a marketing opportunity of my run and pocket a decent amount of money right from the get-go of my career, but that wasn't what I stood for. I was turned off by commercializing the experience and, for that matter, by the running-and-fitness market in general. By seeking publicity for the run and the record, I would have been participating in the very aspect of running that I despised. I had initially thought that would be part of why I was doing the run. But doing the run changed everything. The last thing I wanted was to diminish my experience by endorsing a power bar.

If anyone cared to check, there was proof I ran it in fifty-eight days, as I had signed and dated all the registers I passed. But I didn't want to find out what it meant to someone else, because I knew what it meant to me. And, inevitably, someone would say that my pace was impossible and that I must have scoped out the registers and driven the highway, hiking in at points and signing the registers.

I felt a sense of accomplishment, but not in the modern way. Some people actually feel a sense of accomplishment when they take a plane halfway around the world. They've traveled far to a foreign land. But what have they accomplished? When you can take a journey on your own body power—a mile, 10, or 1,727 in this case—that is an ultimate sense of accomplishment.

Some people want to learn what they are capable of, but they never push their limits to find out. I had done that. Though I had lost fifteen pounds, I felt no joint or muscle pain. I had gone through one pair of modified running shoes. The only problem I encountered was a queasy stomach the final week—which that hubcap of a pancake didn't help. The most interesting physical change was that my feet spread out as if they had been flattened by a truck. I later figured out that my shoe size went from 10.5 to 12.5. As my mileage decreased over the ensuing months, the size returned to normal.

On the final morning, I awoke with one question on my mind. "Am

I doing this run for me or for others?" The goal had essentially been accomplished: I had run it faster than anyone ever had. I didn't want to plant a flag with my name on it as a challenge to others to beat my time. I was actually pleased that I had concluded that the goal was somewhat hollow, for it was the trails of the mountains that were the experience, not the end point.

I had made my decision. I packed up and ran fifteen miles toward the Oregon border. Less than two miles from the state line—the finish line to the California section of the Pacific Crest Trail—I stopped.

I felt joy and humility, but most of all respect for the land and for myself. I took a deep breath, the best of the entire trip. And then rather than run the two miles to the border, I turned around and ran fifteen miles back to Seiad Valley. That afternoon, I caught a bus back to Seal Beach.

In making that decision, I eliminated any chance for commercialism. I decided not to formally cross the finish line. Anyone who bothered to check all the PCT logs from Campo to the Seiad Valley would see that I had run nearly all of the PCT in record time. But nobody would check, because I hadn't signed the final log. Partly, I was being defiant. The border was just an artificial line. But mostly, I was showing that I had done it for myself.

Chapter Eight

HEALTHY AS A HORSE

I 'm not Superman. I'm not even Tarzan, though I would like to believe we have a few things in common. Much of my initial approach to surviving in the wild was rooted in athleticism and my belief in my abilities. Being a runner and approaching survival from that place allowed me to see amazing locations. However, the better I was able to slow down and observe, the more I saw that I needed to become more patient and less reliant on my physical abilities to become a true survivalist.

The more I learned, the clearer it became that the books describing hunter-gatherers spending two hours a day gathering plants and cooking them up were fiction. It became apparent to me that surviving on any landscape takes all day. There is no way to run through an environment and understand it, no matter how fit you are.

Surviving in the wilderness takes an extraordinary amount of patience. But the body has to first adapt to extreme settings, to endure temperature swings, to cover great distances without proper hydration, and to summon deeply stored energy when near collapse in order to reach for that next stage.

The biggest obstacle for most people is the temperature swings. There are numerous tragic stories about raw mountain skiers being lost for days and freezing to death before being found, and there are equally as many stories of day hikers suffering from heatstroke or even heat-induced heart attacks.

From talking to medical professionals versed in survival in dire conditions, I have learned that the first part of surviving in extreme situations is oxygen delivery. The better the body can deliver and process oxygen, the greater the chances both for survival in life-threatening situations and for being able to operate when the body is pushed to its limits.

Dr. Sam Parnia, a noted critical-care physician and bestselling author, explains: "What has happened in Matt and others with his conditioning is that their lungs and heart have adapted to be able to maximize the use of the oxygen that they are taking in. Their breathing has become more efficient with time, and they are taking in more air for every breath than a normal person. Their heart is contracting so much more strongly that for every beat, they are pushing out more blood and more hemoglobin, which carries the oxygen to all parts of the body."

The ability to process oxygen more rapidly helps the body in numerous ways, from increasing endurance to preventing disorientation and cramping from dehydration at high altitudes. Altitude sickness is caused by low oxygen pressure at high altitudes. Elevations at which the effects are felt vary from person to person. Generally, people will feel some change in their breathing around four thousand feet. Above eight thousand feet, most people experience a shortness of breath and the inability to draw enough oxygen to compensate. Activities that cause the body to demand more oxygen, such as skiing or running, compound the problem and often leave people feeling dizzy, sick to their stomachs, or headachy.

The more fit a person is, the better they will be able to deliver and process oxygen at high altitudes. I have met several ultra-distance runners who are as fit as me and can run for long distances in the mountains.

The most amazing runner is Matt Carpenter. Ultra-distance runners often call him superhuman. On top of being genetically gifted, he has built his life around extreme running. In the wintertime, he relocates his family from Colorado to South America so he can live on a high peak and train year-round. Matt has won every high-altitude race numerous times and holds virtually every course record, including the fastest times recorded in marathons run at the unthinkable altitudes of fourteen thousand and seventeen thousand feet.

Carpenter's ability to process oxygen, known as VO2 max, is unparalleled. At the U.S. Olympic Training Center, it was registered at 90.2, the second highest on record behind a Norwegian cross-country skier. A reading of 60 is considered excellent for an athlete.

Though I have never had my VO2 max measured, I doubt it would match Carpenter's. However, once in a routine physical, a doctor was measuring my oxygen saturation level, which is the amount of oxygen in the blood. Anywhere from 95 to 100 percent is normal, depending on a variety of circumstances, such as altitude. The doctor explained that because we were at 5,800 feet, the highest possible reading would be 97. She turned to the machine and said, "And yours is . . . oh my . . . ninety-eight."

I once ran a high-altitude ten-mile race in Colorado against Matt Carpenter. The race had forty superstrong distance runners, including a world-renowned Kenyan runner, and was by invitation only. Entrants had to apply and send a résumé. Because the race was being held at fourteen thousand feet in snowy conditions, I had to trade out my sandals for running shoes. I knew that if I were sloshing through snow in my sandals it would slow me down. I found a pair of Nikes that were low cut and didn't have too high a heel and trained in them for a week before the race.

The race started at eight thousand feet. The Kenyan runner bolted off the starting line at a five-minute-mile pace. All of us, including Carpenter, let him go. He was sprinting at an out-of-this-world pace for an altitude that high, particularly considering we had ten miles to run.

After a couple miles, the group started spreading out. Matt eased past the Kenyan runner and took the lead. I was in fifth place. As we got higher up the mountain, my strength started to kick in. I passed the Kenyan runner, who was by now huffing and puffing in the altitude, and settled into third place.

I felt strong. When we did the turnaround to go down the first mountain, I was tearing it up. I actually had my sights on Carpenter. I thought I might not beat Matt that day, but I was certain I could pull off a second-place finish—which would have given me a big paycheck and a free flight to Italy.

As I charged down the hill, I saw a mountain biker who was preparing to ride up the hill toward the second peak. He was clicking pictures of me. For a split second, I lost my concentration. My running shoes had that small heel, making me less stable, and I rolled my ankle.

It wasn't bad, so I kept running. But after another mile, I was wincing. I thought, *I might be able to finish this race, but I will likely hurt myself.* So I stopped.

Carpenter ended up winning by ten minutes. I didn't have the fitness to catch him, but I felt like I could've beaten the other runners and finished second. Second place to Matt Carpenter is the best you could ever hope for.

While enhanced oxygen delivery can make you feel superhuman, there are other health factors that come into play in extreme situations. Toxins in the body often prevent it from working at peak level. The primary sources of toxins in our body are food, stress, lactic acid in muscles, and poor air, as well as electromagnetic toxins from computers and cell phones. Living in the wilderness strips away the toxins faster and more completely than a massage at a day spa. The natural climate reboots the body over time and leaves it free of toxins that handicap the body's functions and ability to quickly recuperate.

The lack of bacteria and germs in nature also means that I never get sick when I am out in the wild. In city atmospheres, people are exposed to germs and bacteria that cause viruses such as colds and flu. People are constantly washing their hands and using antibacterial products to kill germs. Those types of bacteria don't exist in the wild.

Diet plays an important role in the ability to endure extremes. The Paleo Diet is now in vogue. The basic philosophy of the diet is to eat the way hunter-gatherers ate hundreds and thousands of years ago in pre-agriculture days. The prescribed foods are things that are found in the wilderness such as meats, fish, leafy greens, fruits, nuts, vegetables, and seeds, rather than processed foods and grains or anything with refined sugar. This translates into high protein, low carbohydrate, high fiber, and a much higher intake of vitamins and antioxidants.

Balancing your diet is just as critical. Over the years, I found that eating only plants and grains did not provide me with enough energy to get through the day. I added fish to my diet, but I was still drained and tired. Eventually, I began hunting wild game and eating meat, and my sustained energy level was far higher.

I later consulted the nutritionist Ryan Koch about how I felt. "In a realistic primitive-living situation (the same situation that our ancient human ancestors found themselves in for more than two million years until the Neolithic era around ten thousand years ago), it has been my assertion that a person *must* procure animal foods to remain in good health," Ryan said. "Not only that, but anybody in a primitive setting will *crave* the essential nutrients found *only* in meat and especially fat if they are out there long enough (animal forms of fat-soluble vitamins A, D, and K). In other words, plants will not sustain any lengthy wilderness survival sojourn."

Perhaps the biggest asset to having more strength and endurance has been slowing down my metabolism. This means that I don't have to eat as often. Most Americans eat constantly, or at least three times a day. If they don't eat every five hours, their blood sugar drops and they start to feel woozy.

The fact that my metabolism is slower also helps me store energy in the event I can't find food for a day or more. A slower, more efficient metabolism means that even if I don't eat for a couple days, my blood sugar will remain stable and my energy level won't flatline. Like the Tarahumara, it also allows me to run great distances without needing to consume thousands of calories.

My lifestyle and my fitness constitution have merged. Though I didn't seek publicity, people in the running community took notice of how I lived and trained. *Trail Runner* magazine wrote an article about me.

"Matt Graham is what you might call a traditional runner, but not in the sense of old school legends of the sport like Bill Rodgers or Steve Prefontaine," the article said. "Graham trains like the ancient foot messengers of southwestern Native American tribes, running in homemade sandals and living off the land. He makes jerky out of coyote and raccoon, flint knaps spear points and arrowheads, rubs two sticks together and makes fire. He runs in sandals made of discarded tires or rawhide and yucca fibers. On long runs, he shuns manufactured energy bars for the natural energy from Pinole and chia seeds."

All of this helps explain why I would enter a twenty-five-mile horse race—without a horse.

It was a temporary job in Utah that resulted in a study of a biped versus a quadruped. A friend had asked me to help him and his wife do a traditional Dutch oven cookout for a group of trail riders in the mountains. When we got to the camp to set up, I realized that the group of riders was preparing for a horse race on Boulder Mountain. I cooked and talked with the riders.

The race was a three-day, fifty-five-mile event, with the middle day of twenty-five miles being the toughest. The trail headed southeast and then cut through the mountainous Utah terrain and picked up the old mail route. The trail crossed the Escalante River and headed upstream about five miles to an area called Big Flat, and then wound its way back into the town of Escalante. I was familiar with the route, as I had run it many times.

I started to think that it would be cool to run the race against the horses. I hadn't been on a long run in a few weeks, and the challenge was irresistible. The race had three legs over three days through canyons and over mountains, and the riders could switch horses.

I sought out the race director, a man named Krocadoomis, and asked him if I could enter the middle day—on foot.

Krocadoomis was a classic Southern Utah cowboy with a floppy mustache and ragged hat. He looked at me like I was crazy. He asked how in heaven's name I proposed to keep up against a group of horses.

"With my feet, in my sandals," I replied.

"You won't be able to keep up," he said.

I smiled. "I think I'll be all right."

I convinced him that I knew the land well. Even if the horses blew me away, I wouldn't get lost.

As he thought about it, a smile broke out across his face. He tugged at his mustache. No doubt he was thinking that the local papers might write about the sandaled runner against the thoroughbreds, which could help publicize his business. He agreed that I could run, but set down one condition. At the start, I had to run ahead, open the gate, and either stand aside or take off to avoid the charging horses, which would have a lot of built-up adrenaline in the beginning.

The next morning, I put on a pair of thin sandals with rubber soles made from old VW bus tires and lined up with thirty-seven horses and riders. A few of the riders had gotten to know me from the cookout. I had told them about running the Pacific Crest Trail, though I think only a few of them actually believed me. In any event, they were an eclectic bunch of cowboys and wealthy adventure seekers who weren't about to let a guy in sandals outrun their horses.

Krocadoomis signaled me. I ran about a quarter mile to the gate and opened it. Instead of waiting, I took off down the trail. I could hear the horses pounding. I reasoned the best way to avoid the stampede was to sprint the first couple miles and build a lead while the horses spread out. I kept running through the pine trees. After another mile, the pounding was becoming fainter and fainter. I was actually pulling away from the horses.

On the first leg, we ran down from the mountains into Boulder, about eighteen miles. The terrain favored the horses. There were sandy uphill climbs and some rocky patches that were relatively easy for horses to find their footing. Even the flats were mostly sandy. I assumed the horses could do twenty miles per hour in the flats. Nevertheless, I hadn't seen or heard a horse since the starting line.

When I got into town, I stopped at the rodeo grounds, the designated end point of the first leg. I waited and waited for the horses. I couldn't believe I was that far ahead. The race monitors weren't even there yet. I sat for about twenty minutes until people started showing up with trailers to move the horses to the starting point of the second leg. They were dumbfounded that I was already there. One asked how long I had been there. I told him. He marked my time for five minutes earlier than when he had asked.

Several minutes later, the first horses arrived. It took another fifteen minutes for all the horses to come in. The horses were loaded onto the trailers and driven to the other side of town.

At the second starting point, the race officials let me go first, but they released the horses almost immediately, stripping me of my lead. Once again, I heard the horses pounding behind. I picked up the pace and soon lost them.

I took off running, built a lead, and didn't see a horse until about mile fourteen. I was crossing a canyon and the horse was on the other side, where I had come down minutes earlier. At mile sixteen, I stopped at the vet check station.

The race officials told me that Krocadoomis, who was riding with the race contestants, had radioed in and told them to stop me. "We're not going to vet check you, but we have to hold you for the time it takes to vet check the horses," the guy told me. "To make it fair . . ."

Krocadoomis and several other riders arrived about fifteen minutes later. We talked for a while, and then they let me go. Again, twenty minutes or more had gone by, and they released the horses right after me. I was beginning to think Krocadoomis didn't want me to win.

It was just nine miles to the finish line. The challenge for me was that the final leg of trail was a flat, sandy road. The sand gave the horses a decided advantage. After a mile or so, Krocadoomis and one of the horses passed me.

At some point, I must have zoned out because I ended up taking a wrong turn. When I realized I was not on the race trail, I reversed course. By the time I had rejoined the trail, two more horses had passed me. They were about a hundred yards in front of me. Down the homestretch, it was three stallions, followed by me, and then the other thirty-four horses.

Most humans would have been fine with that performance, but I was determined to retake the lead. The trail came to a cliff with a steep drop-off—the one chance for me to make up some ground on the horses. I raced down the hill, foot over foot, bouncing off rocks like they were rubber, and I managed to pass one of the horses. At the bottom of the hill, there was a half-mile horse-racing track that led to the finish line. I sprinted my absolute hardest, but I wasn't able to catch the first two horses.

I ended up finishing third with a cumulative time of six hours, fifty-seven minutes.

My achievement was respectable, but certainly not unparalleled. Each year, there is a Man Against Horse Race in Prescott, Arizona. The fifty-mile race covers various terrains, including steep mountain climbs and flat plains. Some years a horse wins, but most years a man wins. In another, the Man versus Horse Marathon in Wales, UK, a man has won twice in thirty-five years.

So how can a man outrun a horse?

Stride and breathing are the two main factors. In experiments where a man runs alongside a horse at the same pace, it has been determined that the man's stride is actually longer than the horse's stride. This means that the man's legs are moving slower to cover the same amount of ground, therefore allowing him to cover more distance per stride and conserve energy.

Horses are quadrupeds. Once all four legs are working in unison in a gallop, the horse can't pant. Because panting is the only way for the horse to cool down, a horse in a gallop is constantly heating up. Eventually, the horse will have to slow down to a trot to cool off.

Humans, of course, are bipeds. Even when we reach our "galloping" speed, we can pant. Therefore, even if we are sprinting for a long period of time, we are able to continually cool down enough to keep running.

In the race I ran against the horses, I basically sprinted the entire way. This allowed me to take advantage of stride and breathing. The temperature was in the seventies, so I didn't overheat. To stay light, I didn't carry water. I stopped and drank whenever I found water and at the mandatory stops. I also plucked pine needles off the trees to provide me with a constant stream of energy. The horses ate only when they were at the vet check stops.

Terrain is also a critical factor in a man-versus-horse race. The horse will excel on flat, sandy road; whereas a runner will have an easier time on a narrow trail with several switchbacks mixed with long, flat terrain where the horse will need to rest. That accounts for the difference in the results between the hilly Prescott race and the flat-road Wales race.

The evening after my race, there was a dinner for all the riders. When Krocadoomis spoke, he singled me out. He presented me with a silver medallion.

"When I saw you charging down the canyon and coming up the other side, I finally understood how Geronimo could do it," he said.

EPIC SURVIVAL RULE #3:

KNOW YOURSELF

I am finding that learning survival is a complex process that is as much mental as it is physical. I realize that knowing myself is just as critical to surviving in dangerous situations as being able to endure nature's tests.

Though I know quite a bit about living in the wilderness, I am also just now discovering that survival is a full-time pursuit. The hunter-gatherers we read about in books or see on television look like they are working at it a few hours a day. They throw up a shelter, grab plants on the go, and cook up an occasional meal. But that's not realistic. It takes all day to survive in the wilderness. I no longer believe it is possible to scoop ice cream eight hours a day and be a hunter-gatherer after work and on the weekends.

My approach to the wild has been from an intensely athletic point of view, but I am altering that approach. When I was younger, being a runner allowed me to see many amazing places and work on my hunter-gatherer skills at the same time. That was my identity. But I am trying to find a balance where running great distances does not define me.

I am learning that the ability to slow down is equally as important as running sixty-five miles across a desert in one day. I am beginning to observe more. I don't think I have been missing the grandeur of nature or even the smallest flower petal, but I know that observation is going to be critical to shaping my life as a hunter-gatherer.

Now that I am fully engaged in the process, I realize that it takes an extreme amount of patience. I need to be able to call upon my patience so that I do not make a fatal move, such as trying to seek a shelter I cannot reach when a biblical storm is approaching.

The things I am discovering cannot be picked up from reading a book, and they are critical for me to learn. In every-day life, it is easy to get caught up in yourself. The land does not allow that. It demands that you look around and observe.

As I transition into the land and begin to more fully under-stand it, I am also learning about myself. I want to reach the point where I know myself so well that I can use that in my relationships. I want to be able to pause and ask myself, "Okay, what does my friend need today? What do I need to do to be better for this person?" *For me, being able to do that will mean that I know myself.*

Chapter Nine

FINDING MY PLACE

As a kid, I was always exploring or climbing. *(Personal collection)*

The pit house in the community of Salt Gulch, Utah, that I built and lived in for five years. *(Donna Simpson)*

In the Panama jungle, filming *Dual Survival*.
(Russell Fill)

Preparing to hunt with the atlatl and dart.
(Russell Fill)

On the road for a *Dual Survival* shoot.
(Russell Fill)

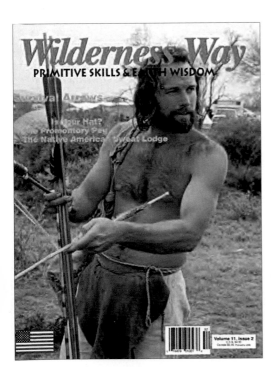

On the cover of *Wilderness Way*.

Addressing a group of students.
(Ace Kvale)

Starting a fire as the Fremont Indians did using the hand drill technique. *(Ace Kvale)*

A small coal is nurtured and brought to life with a gentle breath. *(Ace Kvale)*

The picture shows the focus in the instant the arrow is released. *(Ace Kvale)*

Three atlatls made by me and two darts made by A.J. Applying artistry and attention to detail creates an extension of the maker of the tool. *(Personal collection)*

Blistering sunset over the Kaiparowits Plateau. *(Personal collection)*

Rainwater filtering through and running on top of slick rock in the southern Utah canyons. *(Personal collection)*

This shot illustrates the powerful life-giving energy that storms can generate over southern Utah. *(Personal collection)*

The geological process sculpted by nature over thousands of years. *(Personal collection)*

In the summertime the canyons of Utah can reach over a hundred degrees, but in the wintertime they are blanketed with snow under freezing temperatures. *(Personal collection)*

This image illustrates how flash floods can carve out canyons over time. Despite the cottonwood trees, there is no surface water. *(Personal collection)*

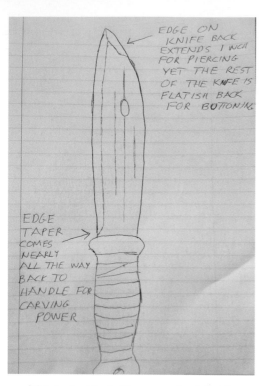

EDGE ON KNIFE BACK EXTENDS 1 INCH FOR PIERCING YET THE REST OF THE KNIFE IS FLATISH BACK FOR BUTTONING

EDGE TAPER COMES NEARLY ALL THE WAY BACK TO HANDLE FOR CARVING POWER

This is the ideal, all-purpose bush knife that I have used for many years.

(Personal collection)

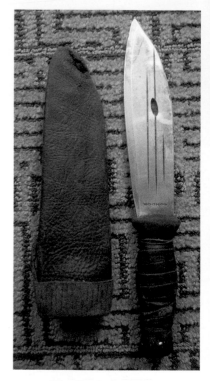

The finished product.

(Personal collection)

On a walkabout in the southwestern United States.

(Personal collection)

The inescapable grandeur of the Grand Staircase-Escalante National Monument hit me harder than any sight I had ever seen. Its beauty is absolute at every turn.

Situated between the small town of Escalante, Utah, and the even smaller town of Boulder, Utah, the Monument, as locals refer to it, is splayed out over 1.7 million acres, making it larger than Delaware. The Monument has three main areas: the Grand Staircase, the Kaiparowits Plateau, and the Canyons of the Escalante. The ever-changing geology is the triumphant result of ancient glaciers and flowing natural waters. A maze of canyons carved out over thousands of years is lined with streams and vegetation. The canyons are hemmed in by dark orange cliffs that transition to reddish-orange plateaus.

Distances are hard to gauge. From the peak of Boulder Mountain at eleven thousand feet, it's difficult to tell if you're looking out a mile or ten.

The mountains have horizontal stripes that look like they were drawn with hundreds of colored pencils. The flats are layered in shades of gray and green that appear to have been mixed together and applied with a paintbrush. The tones and hues of the landscape change constantly with the movement of the sun and placement of the clouds.

Highway 12 passes through the Monument and connects Boulder and Escalante. This section was dubbed the "Million Dollar Road" for the cost of building it in 1935—back when that was a lot of money for a blacktop road. Looking out in the distance from the higher ridges, there is certainly a million-dollar view. The winding road looks like a dark ribbon running along the silhouette of the plateau. In one section of S-curves with no guardrails, called the Hogsback, the ridge is about three feet wider than the roadway.

People often talk about the real world. To me, a place as natural as this is the real world, and the cities we live in are the artificial world. When I first saw the area, I knew I was home.

I moved to the Boulder area in March 1996. I first read about it in a magazine. I was living in the Sierra mountains studying primitive skills when I came across a tiny ad in *Backpacker* magazine for a survival school. The ad had a small arrow with a stone point and read "primitive skills and survival school." There were no pictures. I immediately thought, *That's the kind of place I am looking for.*

I dialed the number of the Boulder Outdoor Survival School (BOSS) and reached the owner, David Wescott. After we spoke for a while, I asked him if he would hire me. He chuckled and explained that I had to take a course before I could work for him. I told him about my lifestyle, and he encouraged me to come to Boulder.

Wescott was in his mid-forties and had worked as an instructor himself. In addition to owning BOSS and another survival school in Idaho, he also hosted the two largest annual gatherings for survival enthusiasts, Rabbitstick in Idaho and Winter Count in Arizona. He was also the cofounder of the *Bulletin of Primitive Technology*, a forum for people who want to share and learn primitive-living skills. I decided that working for him was ideal for me.

I didn't own much. I loaded everything I owned into saddlebags and strapped them on my mountain bike. My parents dropped me at the California-Nevada border on their way to a vacation, and I started pedaling for Boulder, Utah.

The journey was over five hundred miles, across the entire state of Nevada. I was so anxious to get to Boulder that I rode about 130 miles a day, which was the maximum I could do at that time with all the hills.

I rolled into Boulder in mid-March, before the hiking season began, and rode straight to the BOSS office. The only guy there was an instructor named Rob Withrow. He informed me that Wescott would be back in a few weeks. Rob was living in the office during the winter. He was a craftsman who built tools. He told me he was preparing to head up the mountain and live off the land for a while. I asked if I could join him, and he told me to be ready to go the following morning.

I set up camp near the survival school. When I arrived at the office the next morning to see if Rob was ready to leave, he told me he needed more time to get ready. He told me to check back in three days. In the interim, I decided I needed to orient myself with the land.

I climbed to the top of a nearby mesa to a large rock formation called Schoolhouse Ledge. I built a ten-foot circle of stone, where I planned to stay for four days and four nights. I went into the circle wearing nothing but a cotton sheet. I didn't bring any food or water. Like the Indians who went on vision quests, I was seeking clarity for my path forward.

Though I didn't experience any significant visions, I did succeed in readjusting my body to the land. I ended up staying only three days, but those days forced me to slow down, listen to the land, and allow it to open up to me. When I was sitting in the circle, I also found my new home.

In the distance, I could see a dark spot on an otherwise luminous rock formation. I was intrigued. Upon leaving the stone circle, I hiked across the canyon and up the mountain to examine the spot. It turned out to be a hole in the rock the size of a large door. I entered and crawled through a passageway. I went about ten yards and the passageway angled up slightly. Suddenly, it opened into a spacious cave. I decided to make the cave my home.

To this day, it was unlike any cave I've found in the area. It was very heat efficient. In fact, one time I was in the cave sleeping on a cotton sheet. I woke up and there was a bunch of snow on the ground surrounding me, but I was hot and toasty in there.

In just a few weeks' time, I knew that Monument offered me everything I wanted. There were areas where somebody without a lot of experience in survival, provided they knew a few basic things, could live well off the land for a period of time. That was what I hoped to teach others.

Becoming a survival school instructor was more difficult than I realized. When David Wescott finally returned, he explained to me that he had ten people applying to be instructors, but before any of us were hired, we had to pass a rigorous, fourteen-day survival training course.

I felt confident I would do fine. In addition to studying primitive skills on my own, in the month that I was waiting to meet Wescott, I met a local named David Holladay. He was an aficionado of the area, and he taught me about its riches and peculiarities. But I became a little concerned when everyone was packing for the trip.

The other guys were bringing far more supplies than me. I had my traditional five-foot piece of cloth rolled up and tied around my waist. I was wearing a breechcloth and a cotton shirt and sandals. The other guys were all in nylon pants, carrying fully loaded backpacks. They were also packing a second bundle that would be dropped off to us midway through the course. The idea was that after you endured the first part, the second bundle arrived to make you more comfortable. The second bundle contained food rations of nuts and lentils, a poncho, and a blanket.

Breck Crystal, an instructor I had met a few days earlier, asked me where all my gear was. I told him that my rolled-up cloth was all I had. He offered me his extra poncho and blanket.

The course, I soon learned, had phases. I hadn't read the brochure, so I didn't know how it worked. It started with the most challenging part, Impact. In this phase, we walked through the Monument for six days and ate very little. The only water we drank was what we found. We also only ate food we found, like spiderwort, wild onions, mustard greens, and yucca flowers. The idea behind Impact is to force the body into starvation mode. It also readjusts your metabolism. Because we consumed so few calories for those days, during the rest of the course, when we ate eight hundred or more calories a day, it felt like more than enough.

I handled Impact with relative ease. I felt a little light-headed at times. Some of the participants had mini-blackouts when they stood up. As the days progressed, everyone moved slower. Oftentimes when people sat down, it took them a while to get to their feet.

The second phase was Group Expedition. The primary focus of this phase was to teach students how to work with a map and compass, and how to cook. I told the instructors that these were all skills I knew inside and out already and that I was there mostly for the land connection. They only half believed me, but they did allow me to run off and do my own thing during that phase. They became somewhat convinced I knew what I was doing. I would glance at the map in the morning and then run off and meet up with them at the end of the day in a designated spot miles away. I was able to find them by reading the land features and gauging the twists and turns of the canyons.

In the next phase, called Sheep Processing, we processed a sheep that was brought to us. The premise was that students are removed from the meat they buy in the market and grill. A sheep was supposed to more closely represent what they might buy in a market, as opposed to wild animals like squirrels or raccoons. It also showed them how in the processing of a large animal you can use the skin for blankets and the bones to make knives, awls, or tools.

The instructors made an overly elaborate ceremony out of the slaughter. The sheep was placed on its side, and everyone was told to put their hands on the sheep. One person was designated to kill the sheep with a knife. Not only was this unnatural, the person with the knife was so nervous that he barely made the kill without the sheep suffering.

The process made me uncomfortable. I had been on a Navajo reservation and seen sheep sacrificed. The Navajo held a much different ceremony for the animal. One person would lead the sheep. As soon as everyone was distracted celebrating the life of the sheep, the guy leading the sheep would kill it in an instant.

Does the lesson have value for students? Yes, it does help them connect to what they eat. But at the time, I was 100 percent a hunter-gatherer. I never bought meat from a market. Any meat I ate, I hunted, so I had a hard time participating in the killing of a farm animal.

After the sheep was dismantled, no one wanted the fat so I kept it. The fat proved to be a great benefit for the next phase, the Solo. They dropped us off for a couple nights. We each were given a one-quarter-mile section of the canyon and told to stay in that vicinity and build a camp. For food, I picked cactus and fried it in the sheep fat, giving me far more tasty meals than the others had.

The final phase was called Student Expedition. We were given an eighteen-mile route to navigate. The lead instructor's confidence in my skills had grown so he designated me to lead to the starting point. After we all returned, there was one final challenge: a seven-mile run to finish off the course.

Of the ten people, Wescott hired two for the coming season, a woman and me. However, I soon learned that we were not considered full instructors, but rather interns. That summer, I ended up working on seven courses. Each course had seven to ten students and lasted from a week to a month.

At the end of that summer, Wescott sold the school to Josh Bernstein, an Ivy League–educated New Yorker who was well known in the survival skills world. Most of the instructors left town and moved on with their lives, but I stayed. While I hoped to continue working at BOSS under its new owner, the primary reason I stayed was because Boulder was my home.

I had settled on a mesa about six miles outside of town. I built a primitive-living structure called a pit house. I dug a hole nine feet in diameter and about three feet deep, making the pit house deep enough to stand in. The ground was caliche, sedimentary rock that resembles white clay. The caliche was hard enough to enable the sides to stay up without any reinforcement. Most of the soil in the country is sand, which would have needed to be reinforced or turned into cement to achieve the same result.

I built a crib-style roof that spiraled around to a center point and had an opening at the top. I covered the roof with sticks and bark, and packed caliche on top. The pit house was big enough to sleep in with a tiny fire burning alongside me.

I regularly went on walkabouts to explore the land. Shelter was easy to find in the numerous caves. Some of the caves were bigger than small buildings. They measured as much as seventy yards across and had high ceilings, making them big enough to throw a dart the entire length. These were particularly helpful in monsoon season, because even if I had a group of a dozen students with me, it didn't feel claustrophobic.

The caves were made by water. Every time water hits the bank, it carves deeper and deeper into the rock, and eventually you are left with a shelf that is protected. They all have sandy floors in the front near the overhang, but in the back they have non-broken-down oak leaves. These leaves are perfect for making a bed with very little work. They will also keep you warm, as the canyons do get cold at night, particularly in the winter.

Most of the caves are safe. But even if the caves have big boulders, then you can look up at the ceiling to gauge if there is a risk of falling rock. If you see cracks or loose rock, you avoid that spot. But even in caves with unstable parts, there is always a safe section. If there is a pile of rocks, typically the ceiling will have a fissure in that area, but if you proceed to a section where the ceiling is smooth sandstone with no fissure, that area will not fall apart.

The caves tend to sit twenty to fifty feet above the water line. There is a mixture of geology occurring. There are places where a river has cut through and created a cave, but the water is still flowing underneath. Even if a cave has a creek, it is not unusable. Over time, the water will change sides or shift, and a sandy floor will be created.

The land was full of surprises. I was constantly discovering something new. One day, I followed a creek up the mountainside to find the origin of the clear water. I hiked up the mountain about three miles and found a waterfall. The area was a world of its own. There were raccoons and squirrels roaming the land, an abundance of trout in streams, and a bounty of wild greens, such as watercress and mustard.

Because the area is so isolated and difficult to access, nobody ever goes up there. It became one of my retreats, and to this day, I have never seen another person there.

After spending the winter exploring the land, I was eager to begin teaching again. However, the following spring I wasn't rehired at BOSS. Josh Bernstein, the new owner, made changes to BOSS. He replaced many of the guides and didn't bring back any of the interns, myself included.

I ended up spending that summer guiding llama tours. The tours were luxurious by survival standards. Using llamas as pack animals, we would take people into the backcountry, set up camp, cook them meals, and basically wine and dine them. The company used llamas because they are not as temperamental as horses and they are more of a novelty. It wasn't very challenging work, but the tips were generous.

Truthfully, money was never an issue for me. I was earning about two thousand dollars a year, which sounds like a paltry sum but was more than I needed. I broke down my expenses and figured out that I could've easily lived on six hundred dollars a year—not including commercial travel. Half my income went toward going to California to visit family over the holidays.

Eventually, in the summer of 1999, I did go back to work at BOSS. Josh asked me to guide a course with David Wescott, the former owner, who was now guiding. Josh had asked me the previous summer, but I was booked with llama tours. I have to say it felt good to return to showing the land to people who could make their own camp.

At the end of that course, Josh apologized for not keeping me on the previous summer. He even gave me several presents. More important, he hired me as a full instructor. Though I ended up working there for the next eight summers, I soon realized that as well as I knew and loved the land, I was also becoming too rigid and single-minded in my pursuit of connecting fully with the land to become a teacher of its gifts.

Chapter Ten

RELATIONSHIPS

T anning hides is a very meditative exercise. Hunters often discard animal hides, but using them properly fills a part of the cycle of life. When tanned properly, a hide becomes a durable piece of fabric that wears well, has no odor, and is something of a work of art. Wearing animal skins gives you an added connection to the land. There is no way to feel alienated from the natural world with a hide on.

However, if most people saw a fresh hide being skinned from an animal, they would be disgusted. There is a membrane layer like the one on a rack of baby back ribs, only it doesn't peel off quite as easily and it's an inch thick. The hide is covered in blood and pus, with pieces of fat stuck to it. The sight is so gruesome that not even the grittiest movies dare show it.

The smell makes it even less attractive to the uninitiated. In the early phases of the process when I'm stripping down a hide, I find that I breathe so much of the hide that my bowel movements smell like the detritus I peeled off the hide.

In the winter of 1999, I was working the hides of several large animals. I lived in a tepee on a piece of private land in the middle of the National Monument in Boulder. My days were occupied from morning to night with perfecting the hides, but my concentration was spotty at the time, as I felt the pull of a relationship.

I was dating a smart, multifaceted woman named Karen. She was a ranger and had moved to Flagstaff, Arizona, to continue her schooling. We both respected that we had commitments that kept us apart—her education and my work tanning hides.

The fall passed, and we hadn't seen each other for months. At Christmastime, she called me late one night and pressed me to come and live with her. "I need you here, not there," she said.

I told Karen to give me another three weeks. When she protested that that was too long, I told her I couldn't interrupt my project. "I've got to finish tanning these hides," I said in all seriousness. Then I surprised myself by adding, "Maybe we should call it quits."

Undoubtedly, she was thinking, *If Matt's priority is scraping flesh and washing blood off dead animals, then he doesn't love me.* She agreed, and we broke up.

I hung up the phone. A half hour passed. I felt sick to my stomach, far more so that I ever had smelling a hide. I knew what I had done wasn't right. I was being stubborn and selfish, and I quickly began to regret my rigidity. Even the most ancient hunter-gatherers had to factor human interactions into their lives. Maybe it was time for me to do some growing in that area.

So I made a split-second decision to win her back. I decided to leave the unfinished hides behind for my friend to finish. I hurriedly packed a bag, got in my car, and drove through the night to Flagstaff.

I arrived at 8 a.m. the following morning. With a bouquet of flowers in hand, I knocked on her apartment door. A guy answered. Karen heard us talking and rushed to the door. Defensively, she claimed it wasn't what it looked like. But I knew it was—and that I probably deserved it. After all, I had told her I was choosing animal hides over her.

Rather than returning to Boulder right away, I decided to stay on in Flag-staff. I had some money saved up from the guiding season. I had never rented my own place, so I thought, why not try the proverbial "normal life" and see what I could learn? Perhaps it would help me in my next relation-ship, or at the very least in my ability to communicate with my students.

I rented a room in a house and took a job working in a health food co-op. I bought a membership to a climbing gym, and I even signed up for three classes at the community college—theater, anthropology, and dance. There was no stewing about my ex-girlfriend. There was no mo-ment that wasn't full.

At the climbing gym, I became friends with one of the instructors, Jesse Perry, who was an expert climber. On his days off, we climbed routes in the mountains outside of town. Jesse also had an interest in primitive skills. I started teaching him how to make rabbit sticks, hunting boomer-angs, bows, and buckskin pouches and bags. At that time, my belongings were still very primitive. I didn't own any modern gear. Everything was made by hand. He commented that my room looked like a museum.

As spring 2000 drew closer, I decided to return home to Boulder, but I didn't like driving. I had owned a truck camper for four years and only put a total of twelve thousand miles on it, despite the fact that I lived in rural Utah. I decided to leave the truck with Jesse's parents and walk back home for the summer. Jesse asked if he could join me on the walk to see what he could learn about living in the wilderness.

We set out on May 17, 2000. I wore rawhide sandals and carried a wool cloth, tools for flint knapping, a few tablespoons of spirulina—dried algae so complete in vitamins it is called a "superfood"—and a water bottle. Jesse also wore sandals and rolled up all of his supplies, including a mechanical pencil and a blank journal to record our journey, in a cloth. He dubbed his traveling pack "my burrito." We also carried a bow and several reed arrows that I had made.

The route we chose was about 450 miles, roughly 100 miles longer than the driving route. I wanted to try to miss as much of modern civilization as possible. As expected, there were spectacular wilds, but also plenty of things I didn't want to see.

To reach the national forest trails without following the roads, we started out by crossing a vast forest. We were forced to climb over several barbed wire fences separating one plot of private land from the next. With each new area of land came a different pack of barking dogs. As we jogged, ran, and dodged our way through, I felt like exactly what I was—a trespasser. It was not a way to begin a teaching-and-learning experience.

Once we reached the federally protected land, there were more signs of man interacting recklessly with the land. The forestland was dotted with burned ponderosas. The trees served as a reminder of careless campers whose unextinguished fires were all too often sparked by windy, dry conditions and burned through the land.

On the second day, we experienced yet another contrast between the wilds and modern society. We awoke in a sea of aspen and Douglas fir banked by the distant glow of purplish mountains. After we ate thistle roots and cleaned up our campsite, we headed north and ran into Highway 180. We walked along the shoulder for several miles, as cars and trucks roared past us. The shoulder was littered with trash tossed out of car windows, such as Doritos bags, crushed soda bottles, and a torn T-shirt.

We shifted about four miles from the highway and paralleled it. At that point, Jesse felt like we were pushing our dehydration limits. It was early in the journey, but he was uncomfortable. He said he was considering turning around and walking back to the highway. I didn't respond. I pressed on, and he followed.

After another mile, we crossed a dirt road. The tracks were so old and so deep that it was clear that no car had driven on it for months. Sitting on the road right in the exact spot where we crossed was a bottle of Ocean Spray cranberry juice. It had been sitting there so long that the label was completely sun beaten.

I opened the bottle. We both smelled it. Undoubtedly, it was passed its expiration date. We each took a few sips. We realized that it was a little bit on the fermented side, but we decided to carry it with us and drink it later.

I could also see that Jesse's energy level was low. For the first couple days, we had eaten only chia seeds, thistle roots, steamed greens, and pine tree bark. The lack of food and the walking in the hot sun caused Jesse to half joke that he was feeling like he was tripping on psychedelic mushrooms.

His blood sugar was crashing from a lack of calories, and it was taking his spirits down with it. In the middle of the highway, I spotted a dead squirrel. I waited for a break in the traffic and then ran onto the highway and scooped up the squirrel. Not surprisingly, Jesse had never eaten roadkill, but we needed the nutrition.

I took the squirrel into the bushes to clean it. I asked Jesse to hold one end while I held the other. As I began to cut off the head with my knife, the look on Jesse's face told me he wasn't going to eat the animal, regardless of how desperate he was for the calories.

Jesse had grown up as a vegetarian. Eating meat was something he didn't want to take part in, but ultimately he knew that he would need to in a survival experience. But he was not ready to make the compromise, which I fully respected.

As our journey continued, Jesse continued to face the same dilemma. He was coming to the conclusion that he could not exist on chia seeds and greens. Food—particularly that which would be classified as vegetarian—was at a premium.

At one point, I managed to get a rabbit with the bow and arrow Jesse was carrying. I skinned the rabbit and cooked it up. Jesse was disgusted. Not only did he not eat any of the rabbit; he threatened to leave at that very moment.

"I don't feel like this trip is for me," he said.

I was sympathetic. I told Jesse that I understood how he felt. I asked him if he would at least continue with me for a few days to see how he felt. He agreed and settled for eating pine nuts that night.

As we continued hiking, I immediately felt stronger. Jesse, on the other hand, was feeling weak, and could see how energized I was. There was a stark difference in our energy levels. Later that day when we made camp, Jesse decided to eat the rabbit meat. He had concluded that there was more to learn.

Though Jesse's beliefs were being challenged, he was also going through the physiology of what happens to human beings when they don't have a lot of food. While their stomach is growling, that is not the real mental challenge. In fact, they are experiencing a flood of emotions they have never previously experienced.

The fact that I had killed and cooked a rabbit was not the issue. It was that he was in a deprived state of being. The feelings are so overwhelming and intense that they fool your mind to the point that you can become depressed because you are seeing and feeling too much. At the end of the range of emotions, when he ate the rabbit, his body equalized and gave him a clearer perspective on what it would take to survive.

That night, we climbed Humphreys Peak, up to some twelve thousand feet. We walked through a forest of aspens. As we headed down off the mountain toward the high desert, it was getting late in the day. Darkness was falling fast. The winds were kicking up. But I made the decision to continue hiking through the night, both to make miles and to drop some elevation.

We weren't dressed to travel in that kind of weather. I was wearing shorts, a buckskin top, and a felt hat. Jesse had on shorts and a cotton shirt. The temperature was in the forties but the wind chill dropped it to the twenties. Temperature-wise we weren't in the danger zone, but we were because of how we were dressed.

We continued walking to make those miles and to stay warm. In survival situations, when it is cold and you have enough visibility, you want to walk because it keeps you warm. However, all the while, it is scary because you know you will have to stop and deal with your survival needs. The dilemma is making sure that when you do stop, you have a clear head.

The light seemed to be coming from an otherworldly source. Every few minutes, places on the desert floor would light up, like sparks jumping off an electrical box. The flashes of light were coming from the ground and going up into the sky. One would be a hundred feet away from us, followed by another thirty feet away, and then another fifty feet in the other direction. Sometimes we both saw the flashes together; other times only one of us would see the flash.

After each flash, we would walk to the spot where it had originated.

When we reached that place, it was just dirt. Granted it was dark, but we never saw an explanation for why a flash of light would be rocketing up from the ground.

When we finally stopped that night out of fatigue, it was pitch-black. There was no moon. Clouds were covering the stars so we didn't have that light, either. It was nearly impossible to see. Feeling my way through our supplies, I pulled out our fire kit. I had packed a hard drill and piece of cottonwood root.

I took the stone knife out and then I started drilling into the board. I couldn't see where to cut the notch, so I had to feel the hole with my finger. I started carving the notch with my stone knife, hoping it was in the right place. I felt back and forth between the notch and the hole. It seemed to be right.

I kept drilling. In the day, when you are making a coal, you can watch for the smoke. But even if there was smoke, I couldn't see it in the dark. I had to wait for the red glow. That added an extra thirty seconds to a minute of drilling.

As I was drilling, I finally saw the salvation: a faint red glow. Jesse brought me some bark and I put it on the nest. I blew the spark into a flame. We then gathered a few sticks and ignited them. That light enabled us to see other wood in the area, which we collected and put on the fire.

After the fire was lit, I looked at the fire board. I realized that the notch wasn't touching the hole. I had been very lucky to get a coal. Normally, if the notch isn't directly in the hole, you cannot get a coal.

Both Jesse and I were grateful for the fire. We spoke only briefly about what a tough night it would have been without the fire. Jesse was on his first survival walkabout. He didn't understand the severity of the situation had I not gotten the fire going. For me, there was no point to take him down that path.

It was our second night out. Jesse was looking at the journey through fresh eyes, so he regarded it as mild drama. Could we have survived the night without a fire? Maybe. But without a doubt, we would have been in the early stage of hypothermia. I had been there before. Likely, I would have survived. I'm not sure about Jesse.

In a survival situation, there are a certain amount of priorities that must be met to stay alive. Sometimes those priorities come one at a time, but other times they hit you all at once. It is easy to get into that kind of predicament. When they hit you all at once, that's when you have to really know the flow of the land. That's when people get into trouble, when there are multiple survival issues that compound themselves. If you don't know how to prioritize those, you will die.

That night, likely because I knew the situation had been dangerous, I began processing thoughts on life issues I needed to address. Before leaving on the trip, I had briefly gotten back together with Karen. We had shared some wonderful moments. But during those first few days with Jesse, as I began sinking back into the land, I regretted that decision. Our relationship had not been a healthy one emotionally.

I knew I was seeing the land in a way she would never be able to comprehend. I was on my own path to become a teacher of the land. I hoped I would find students willing to learn, because I concluded that was more important to me than my own personal relationships.

Chapter Eleven

THE LONG WALK HOME

The major difference between walking from place to place and going on a walkabout is that you cannot avoid roads, people, and pollution. In the National Monument in Utah, I could easily go on a walkabout for a week without encountering any of those because I knew the land. But walking from Flagstaff, Arizona, to Boulder, Utah, despite picking the most remote, backcountry route, I knew that Jesse and I were going to cross roads and find disturbed areas, unregulated mines, and other things that would pain us to see when we were trying to have a very pure connection with the land.

From Flagstaff, Jesse and I walked ninety-five miles across the desert and into Grand Canyon National Park. At the south entrance to the Grand Canyon, we stopped to resupply in Tusayan, Arizona. The town is a bastion of low-end commercialism, and the embarkation point for every conceivable tour of the Grand Canyon—air, foot, bus, bike, mule.

The businesses lining the main drag told the story. Mixed with souvenir shops and "trading posts" were helicopter rental companies, motels, fast-food joints, and a place labeled "The Tourist Center." One motel featured a twenty-foot-tall Fred Flintstone pointing at a sign that read " 'Yabba-Dabba-Doo' Means Welcome to You." I felt anything but.

Tusayan is the home of Grand Canyon Airport, where helicopter and airplane tours of the Grand Canyon originate. At midday in high season, the skies are like LaGuardia Airport on a Friday afternoon. Seeing hundreds of helicopters in the sky eating up the environment and drowning out the natural sounds of the land frustrated me to no end. I felt like I had to do something.

I ran out into a clearing and frantically waved both arms at a low-flying helicopter. After seeing people wave back, I squatted, pointed my backside upward, pulled down my pants, and mooned them. Admittedly, it was not the most mature move, but it was the place I was in.

Jesse certainly didn't mind. In fact, he broke up laughing so hard that he doubled over and ended up rolling on the ground.

Jesse was as disgusted by the noise pollution and hordes of tourists as I was; yet he was also happy to be near civilization. As I set up camp, he jogged into town to buy some comfort food. He returned with two bottles of Guinness and a bag of Oreos.

That night, we were able to ease our frustrations somewhat. I taught Jesse how to make a fire with a small chert, a yucca stick, a few pieces of bark, and some elbow grease to create friction. He was extremely pleased when his efforts produced a wisp of smoke, followed by flames.

Nevertheless, the experiences of seeing trashed areas of the land and helicopters leaving a film of smoke on what would otherwise be one of the cleanest vistas in the country wore on me. I found myself growing bitter and cynical, as well as judgmental and preachy. Our talks focused on what civilization is doing wrong rather than what we can do right. It was bringing me down, and I'm sure it was bringing Jesse down, too.

After we left Tusayan, we hiked to the south rim of the Grand Canyon and stopped for the day. I began making a new pair of sandals. We were within sight of the tourist path, and I could see that many noticed me sitting there, hammering on the yucca fibers with a rock. Jesse joked that they probably thought I was a paid attraction, a frontiersman working away to show how rustic the area once was.

We spent much of the day staring off the rim of the Grand Canyon and enjoying the view. I had us wait until 7 p.m. I figured by that hour the rangers would be off duty and we could just slip into the park before dark, as we did not have a hiking permit.

It was about two hours before dark. We had plenty of light to get into the canyon, but we needed to leave. We started running down the trail. But just as we hit the first turn, we ran into three rangers coming up the trail. They stopped us and asked where we were going.

I told them we were going to Boulder, Utah. The rangers looked uncertain. The lead ranger studied our meager belongings and asked if we were planning to camp in the canyon. They held the fate of this part of our journey in their hands. I smiled at him. "We might take a nap," I said.

The lead ranger nodded. "Have a good trip, guys," he said.

Jesse and I headed into the canyon. We traveled several miles and then slept for the night.

After days of walking through the canyon, Jesse's knee began bothering him. It reached the point where he felt he was going to collapse under his own weight. Considering the dry and rugged crossing that lay ahead of us, we both decided he needed medical attention before continuing.

We made a plan. Jesse would hitchhike his way back to Flagstaff to have his knee checked out. When I reached Marble Canyon, which was about sixty miles away, I would call him and see if he was able to rejoin me.

After leaving Jesse, I spent two days with my friend Farlinger on the North Rim of the Grand Canyon, working on a flint-knapping project. Before leaving, I phoned Jesse. The diagnosis was an inflamed IT band along the outside of his knee. His doctor treated him with acupuncture and bee venom therapy and told him that after a few days' rest he could return.

I set out across the Grand Canyon. I stayed away from the highway that ran north of the canyon. The route was rugged. There were a lot of canyons coming in and out. It was by far the hardest part of the journey. I walked more than thirty miles without any water.

I dropped down off the plateau to a beautiful canyon called North Creek. It was lined with oak trees and full of trout, watercress, and edible greens. Once I reached the bottom, it turned to pure desert. For miles and miles there was only clay. The tallest plants were about six inches. The land was tranquil. The temperature was upward of a hundred degrees. There was no water at all.

In the morning, I would get up as soon as I could see and begin to walk. Even before the sun would crest the horizon, the mercury would start to climb. Once the sun rose, it felt like a fire was searing me. At one point, partway through the walk across the desert, I put on my yucca sandals to start breaking them in because my rawhide sandals were almost worn out.

The first life anywhere close to me was a cottontail rabbit. I thought I should try to get it for food. I picked up a flat stone and threw it with the sidearm motion used for skipping rocks in a stream. I hit the ear of the rabbit. It dropped its head into a crouch and started sprinting. As the rabbit raced away, I picked up another rock and took one more throw. The rock sliced through its throat, killing it instantly.

I didn't have any water, so I couldn't cook the rabbit. I cut it up into strips and hung the meat on a stick with string. It was so hot I figured I would have jerky within a day.

The following day, I entered the Navajo reservation and found a white water tank for cows. There was no surface water, so I climbed up onto the tank to drop my water bottle in and pull out the water. For purification, the only thing I had was grapefruit extract, so I mixed it with the water. The rabbit at that point was bone dry. I enjoyed a meal of jerky with my water.

I didn't have much farther to go. Fueled by the food and water, I hiked longer that day through the desert. As it started to get dark, I saw some lights in the distance. I could see it was the highway paralleling the cliff. I had no idea I was still at least eight miles from Marble Canyon.

Though I had a makeshift map, I was traveling mostly by memory. When I was on the South Rim of the Grand Canyon, I had traced a map of the region that stretched all the way to Marble Canyon. I had included the high points that would be easily identifiable, but there was no way to gauge distances.

I ran toward the lights, covering several miles fairly quickly. I came upon a hotel on the highway before Marble Canyon. As I approached, I saw two Native Americans leaning against a lit-up sign. When I reached them, I stopped and said hello to them.

One of the guys looked me up and down, turned to me, and said, "When I first saw you running out there, I thought you were Forrest Gump. But now that I see you, I know you're a prophet." It was a classic Indian line, mixed with a heavy dose of pop culture.

One of the guys introduced himself as Robert Mirabal. He was from Taos, New Mexico. I later learned that he was a world-renowned, Grammy Award–winning flutist whose flutes have been displayed in the

Smithsonian's National Museum of the American Indian. He explained that the following morning he was heading out on a raft trip on the Grand Canyon. A group was paying him to sit in their boat and play his flute.

We spoke for a while. I told him I had made a flute during the trip. It was the type of flute you blow into from the side. I couldn't play it very well. He looked at me and said, "I can play anything with a hole in it."

Sure enough, he took the flute and made it dance. The music was gorgeous. I was excited because he showed me that my flute had potential to make beautiful music. I vowed to keep practicing it until I was able to play it well.

Robert gave me an elk leather necklace. He said that he had worn it in Hawaii when he performed there. Because he had said he admired elk hide sandals, I took mine off and handed them to him. He told me to stay with him if I ever made it to Taos.

We shook hands. I walked a mile into the countryside to get away from the motel and camped for the night.

The following morning, I met Jesse in Marble Canyon. He was shocked at how tan I was since I had seen him. I told him that the sun had been hotter than I had ever encountered. He openly wondered if he could have made it.

"I have never met anyone who has so much faith that the wild will take care of him," Jesse said.

"If you're being respectful, the wild will take care of you, too," I replied. Then I added, "Let's go."

We continued on our journey to Boulder. There were times that we pushed the envelope by everyday standards, but I felt that because we did, magical things happened and the land opened up to the point where you can't deny that there is a large force taking care of everything.

Jesse was often concerned that we always seemed to be on the edge of dehydrating. At one point, we were down to a quart each. He was constantly concerned that we would run out. But just as the situation felt critical, water would appear. Once it was at a barely functioning desert spring. Another time we were dangerously low, and we ran into a man working for the government. He was making the area livable for bighorn sheep, and he directed us to the water source used for the sheep in drought conditions.

During one stretch when he became discouraged, I asked Jesse what he wanted. He responded that we were near Paria River and he had heard the fishing was good, so some fishing line would be nice. We walked a hundred yards. Sitting on the road was a brand-new spool of fishing line.

He was in shock.

"What else do you want?" I asked.

"Hooks," he said.

Literally in another hundred yards, I found a bag of hooks. He laughed at the absurdity.

"I prefer lures," I said.

Sure enough, we walked another fifty yards and found a bag of lures.

He was speechless. Had we not been in the middle of nowhere, he would have looked around for a hidden camera. Truthfully, I didn't know what to make of those instant gifts, either. That kind of absolute syn-chronicity is rare.

How did it happen? I'm not sure, but it did show that if you have a relationship with the land, it will respond in positive ways. For Jesse, it confirmed that mystical events can happen when you place absolute trust in the land.

The Paria Canyon-Vermilion Cliffs Wilderness had prairielike plateaus interrupted by deep canyons. Though the land was unusually dry, we found a narrow river to follow and it led us to an apricot orchard. We picked a bushel of apricots and made camp. I then built an oven from sandstone slabs and wet clay, and we baked a loaf of apricot bread.

But the area was also teeming with tourists. We passed groups of hikers wearing heavy boots and lugging overstuffed backpacks. The groups seemed to be divided into two schools of thought on us. Some seemed enchanted by our mountain-man appearance, while others cast a wary glance and kept their distance.

Jesse and I debated the experience these hikers were having. He pointed out that before coming out with me he had no idea that the outdoor retail industry had scared the public into believing it needed vast amounts of gear to camp out. He felt that the majority of people were being lulled into believing they were having a wilderness experience when, in fact, they were on something that better resembled a ride at Disneyland and only gave them the illusion of the experience.

Part of this was due to the fact that hikers were supposed to buy a permit to travel through the Paria wilderness and stay on the trails. While I understand this was primarily for safety, it also showed an assumption that the average person could not venture from the predetermined path and learn the wilds for themselves. Though I felt that Jesse's assessment was somewhat harsh, I wasn't sure I would've wanted to see some of the people we passed trying to survive in a remote area.

Once we entered Paria Canyon, we were alone. The canyon was filled with beautiful oak trees and knee-high brush. A narrow river with sandy banks ran through it. Eight-hundred-foot red rock walls towered above both sides of the river. The river was narrow enough that you could jump across it.

My yucca sandals were shot. I had given my backup pair of sandals to Robert Mirabal, so I had to go barefoot. I stuck the yucca sandals in a cave by the river. We joked that someone would find them and think they were archaeological artifacts because they were made in the ancient way. Even the straps were woven from yucca fibers.

I was barefoot. Like a kid at the beach on a summer day, I would run through the hot sand and then cross into the water to cool my feet. I did this for the thirteen miles it took us to reach Big Water.

We sustained ourselves on the apricots and bulrush shoots we gathered along the river. The apricots were a godsend. Without those, we would have both been in trouble because nature was not giving us much during that stretch. Jesse later wrote of our meager meals: "Dreams of pancakes and hash browns carried me through the blood sugar debt of the late afternoon."

After leaving the canyon, we crossed a stretch of desert. Parts were rocky and tough on my feet.

We moved at a pretty good clip because we had a goal in mind: a meal at the café in Big Water. When our reward came into sight, we sprinted to the door, only to be greeted by intense disappointment. The café had closed fifteen minutes earlier.

Jesse laughed and volunteered that we should press on rather than wait until it opened in the morning. The decision was made easier because we knew that we had a drop box waiting for us at the Big Water post office.

We walked across the highway to camp out in the desert for the night. The only food we had came from a ketchup packet we found on the highway. Luckily, it had not been run over. I tore it open and we shared the tomato paste for dinner that night.

The next morning, we went straight to the post office to pick up our shipment.

The town's postmistress was amused by us. "I've been waiting for you two," the small lady said. "For three weeks I've been wondering what's in these two boxes, but mostly, I've been curious who was going to pick them up." By her smile, I guessed that her two new customers did not disappoint her.

My box had a leather bag full of beans and rice, and my tire sandals. Jesse's had a nylon backpack, food, and a water filter. I strapped on my tire sandals. After walking in sandals that were falling apart and then going barefoot for thirteen miles, I was very appreciative to have new footwear.

Jesse and I traveled another fifty miles and reached Last Chance Canyon on June 5. We decided to make it our home for the next week to give us a reprieve from some of the ugliness we had encountered. The worst, which stuck with me, was when we had come upon a spot on an Indian reservation that was trashed. Inconsiderate campers had left bottles and plastic containers, as well as the coal remains from their campfires. We cleaned up the site as best we could.

Located just over the Arizona-Utah border, Last Chance Canyon is hot and dry and extremely remote. We managed to find a nice cottonwood tree to shelter us from the sun. Water was an issue. The streams contained visible cow dung, as ranchers in the area allow their cows to wander the public land. We made the water potable by filtering it through some fine mesh I had brought for such emergency situations.

During our time there, I busied myself with projects in hopes of evoking Jesse's interest. I carved rabbit sticks and made a cloak out of my blanket. Jesse, however, was content to do nothing. He went on a few walks to get a better view of the sunset. He did do some gathering of juniper berries and cooking, but I still felt as if he wasn't attempting to forge a close connection with the land.

After leaving Last Chance Canyon and hiking across the Kaiparowits Plateau, we reached the Canyons of the Escalante. A year earlier, I had buried a stash of food in a large bucket for my trips through the canyon. I located the rock formation. We made digging sticks from a juniper bush and dug for the food.

The journey was in its final leg, and our differing goals for the trip finally came to a head. The following night over a fire, we aired our grievances. I told Jesse I didn't feel he was making a true effort to learn the primitive skills I was teaching him.

He, in turn, explained that he didn't embark on this journey as a student. He simply wanted to live away from the workaday world for six weeks and take in the environment. It was a simple, honest, and straightforward conversation that not only reestablished our friendship but also ended up becoming a building block for me as a teacher.

With our hopes more clearly defined and better understood, the final week of our trip was the best. We spent two days in Choprock Canyon, which offered both of us the reprieve we were seeking. One wall of the canyon had a huge mural of petroglyphs—tiny, detailed pictures carved into the rock depicting an ancient society. The area was filled with cattails and bulrush. The spring water from the creek was the purest of the trip.

We also established a new level of understanding. While sitting in camp, I heard a bird chirp far up in the tangled vines of a tree. I went to investigate. As I climbed up, a bird flew out of a nest. I noticed there were eggs in the nest. As I tried to get my hand into the nest to grab the eggs, the momma bird dove at me and attempted to peck me with her beak. I didn't have any interest in killing the momma bird. I instructed Jesse to grab his rabbit stick to push the momma bird away so she didn't nail me with her beak.

The nest had three eggs. I was planning on us each taking an egg. I reached in and grabbed a small egg and handed it down to Jesse. He refused to take it.

Though I was frustrated, I was beginning to understand his perspective. That moment became a learning experience for me, too. Never again would I consider taking two eggs out of a three-egg nest because I know the momma would abandon the nest.

Three days later, Jesse and I arrived in Boulder on June 23, the eve of my twenty-eighth birthday. After I showed him around my space, we parted ways. Jesse hiked into town to plan his return to Flagstaff.

The trip was a turning point for me in several ways. I realized that I had a weakness as a teacher. I needed to figure out how to bring light to my students, not tear things down in front of them. I had to accentuate the positive of the wilderness in a way they could understand. It couldn't be a simple contrast where nature represented good and man-made represented evil. Even though I saw destructive things, I couldn't focus on the bitterness they evoked. That wouldn't do my life or theirs any good.

I ended up becoming close friends with Jesse. He sent me his diary. Reading his thoughts only underscored the learning curve I was on. The diary made it clear that I was more aggressive when it came to pushing survival concepts and less receptive to him taking them in on his own terms than I needed to be. I had to find a way to better convey the natural world to people willing to learn its gifts. I wasn't yet the teacher I hoped to be.

Chapter Twelve

AN ALL-PRIMITIVE WALK

Ötzi the Iceman was the first all-primitive man discovered by archaeologists. A natural mummy unearthed on the Austria-Italy border, Ötzi was nearly fully preserved and carbon-dated to around 3,300 BCE. He was wearing a coat, a loincloth, tights, and shoes, all made of leather, and a bearskin hat. Around his waist was an ancient fanny pack containing a primitive tool kit of a drill, a bone awl, and flint-knapping tools tipped with copper that were used to shape stones. He was also carrying a copper ax and several arrows made with dogwood shafts.

His shoes became the subject of much debate. Resembling sandals, they were much wider than his feet and appeared to be constructed for walking across snow. The soles were made of bearskin and the sides were animal hide. They were insulated with grass for warmth and had netting around the ankles. What stood out the most was the detail and thought that went into the footwear.

Ötzi was also carrying two species of mushrooms with leather strings running through them. One, the birch fungus, had antibacterial properties and was likely used for medicinal purposes. The second, a tinder fungus, appeared to have been used in conjunction with several plants and some pyrite for fire-starting purposes.

My friend Breck Crystal and I studied Ötzi's possessions in great detail as we prepared to embark on an all-primitive walk. We didn't necessarily want to emulate him, but we did want to show ourselves that we could create tools and supplies like our most ancient ancestors and walk into the wilderness and survive.

Our primitive tool search led us to Ishi, who was considered the last Stone Age American man. He was the last surviving member of the Yahi, a group that was part of the Native American Yana people in California. After living nearly all of his life with no connection to modern society, Ishi emerged in 1911. It turned out that after his entire people were massacred, he had lived completely alone for three years.

Ishi allowed anthropologists and archaeologists to document his way of life, and the methods he had used to survive. After his tribe died, he burned off all his hair in mourning. He fended for himself for years, but with no tribe to back him up, that lifestyle took a toll. He was actually caught stealing eggs, which forced him to come out of the wilderness.

Ishi immediately adapted to the modern world because it was so much easier. After living for a year in the urban world, he said that life became so comfortable for him that he did not want to ever return to the woods. He could eat whatever he wanted, whenever he pleased. He could work on his crafts without the fear of letting down his guard.

Many people I've talked to over the years have the initial impression that the hunter-gatherer lifestyle is a laid-back one. The fact that Ishi was starving to the point where he had to steal eggs shows that even somebody who grew up in that situation has to work so hard for food that they can become desperate. Nature is not cruel; it just cannot be slowed down.

Someone who lives fully in nature cannot say: "I don't think I'll do the hunter-gatherer thing this week. I'm gonna take some time off and get back to it next week." However, in our modern society, we can actually check out of our lives for a couple weeks and then resume them. But if a hunter-gatherer does that, he will die.

Closer to home, Breck and I also studied the Paiute Indians, one of the most fascinating and overlooked Indian tribes. The local Utah Paiute tribe was one of several in the Western states, and all of them had struggled to find and maintain a home. They lived a Stone Age lifestyle all the way through the 1900s.

Though information on the Paiute tribe was sparse, a friend of mine named Bill Latade, an archaeologist who lived in Boulder and was head curator of the Anasazi State Park Museum, had a private manual with photos and historical information. I was interested in their tools but also in their values and customs.

One of the most interesting bits of information I found about the Paiute tribe was their patience and dedication to craft. They made nets out of plants that were hundreds of yards long and stretched them across the plains to catch rabbits. It was the most impressive feat ever seen in a hunter-gatherer tribe.

It took a person roughly one year of constant work to make a hundred yards of the plant-fiber netting. Collecting a fistful of the fibers took several hours. They would then weave them together with their hands and feet, spending a year on one net. The long sections of net were woven just loose enough to trap a rabbit's head. When the nets were not in use for hunting, they were folded over and over to create a well-insulated six-by-six-foot blanket.

The big lesson for us was that a person could find the concentration and patience to twist these fibers with their hands and feet every day for a year.

I also read Father Silvestre Vélez de Escalante's journals. Father Escalante, for whom the nearby Utah town was named, and his companion, another priest, set out to travel from Santa Fe to Monterey, California, in 1776. They ended up in what would become Utah, the first two white men known to have set foot in the state. Father Escalante kept a record of their travels, detailing the survival tools and techniques they used, as well as what they encountered.

The goal that Breck and I had was to take a journey using primitive means. The BOSS season had ended in December 2000, and most of the staff had left Boulder for the winter. The final outing was something of a production. To promote the upcoming *Charlie's Angels* movie, Cameron Diaz, Drew Barrymore, and Lucy Liu had gone on a four-day course as part of a promotional shoot for *Marie Claire*. The three actresses proved they could handle themselves better than many who had taken BOSS courses.

Although it wasn't conscious, the contrast to the journey Breck and I were preparing for was somewhat comical.

Breck and I wanted to enter nature without any connections to the modern world. We both had a foundation for exploring the land, and we wanted to see if we could do it as the ancient explorers had, with only the materials they had used.

To build our primitive tool kit, we absorbed every story we could find, from Ötzi's shoes to Ishi's arrows. We looked at photos and decided what pouches, blankets, and bags to bring, and what foods we wanted to collect and prepare. We referred to Bill Latade's books about the tools the indigenous people of Utah had used to build the area's early living structures, as well as other illustrated books showing how Native Americans made their tools.

For food, we dried jerky and made pemmican, a jerkylike food consisting of dried berries, meat, and fat. The process took two months. We started by drying rose hips and berries. Next, we took deer that had been killed by motor vehicles and left roadside. The dried deer meat was pounded down along with the rose hips and berries. We then heated that up and mixed it with rendered raccoon fat.

The purpose of the fat was to preserve the meat. Rendering animal fat to its purest state keeps it from turning rancid. The fat is rendered in water and then the layers are scraped off. After several processes, only the superwhite fat is left. The white fat is the best. It keeps the meat from going bad and can last hundreds of years. Pure dried meat jerky, in contrast, lasts only about six months before it begins to lose flavor and feel like cardboard.

After rendering the fat and cooking the meat, we rolled the pemmican into small balls that we stored in parfleche. Parfleche is a method of storage for dried food used by Native American tribes. It is made by taking rawhide from an animal, stretching it out tight, and then staking it until it dries. After it dries, the rawhide is pounded with a round cobblestone until it starts to loosen up enough to be folded without breaking.

Our pemmican had just the right mix of meat and sweet berries. It was high in nutrients and tasted far better than it should have. That was actually a mistake. The pemmican was so good that it was hard not to eat it right away. Before we even started, our supply began to dwindle.

Along with the deerskins from the roadkill, we also collected deerskins from hunters (as they discard the skins). We processed the skins and made loincloths, vests, shirts, shorts, and moccasins. I tanned a full-size elk and made a blanket. We also wove together yucca and agave fibers to create the nets for our iceman packs. I made a pack very similar to Ötzi's, while Breck made a more modern design in the shape of an X.

To cook our food, Breck made a clay pot and I hollowed out a gourd and oiled it really well so I could use a hot rock in it. We made our own knives out of stone and put shiny, wooden handles on them. We used the tanned skins for sheaths and sewed them with yucca fibers.

For hunting tools, I made a bow out of hickory with sinew backing for extra strength. We made our own arrows with stone tips. The bow-string was made out of the tendons from the deer. Those same tendons were used to tie the fletching—the guiding feathers—onto the arrows. The shaft was built with cane I had collected in Arizona and some tamarisk, a heavy wood that resembles a willow.

We went overboard on the footwear. We figured that if Ötzi had made snowshoes more than five thousand years ago, we as modern hunter-gatherers should have footwear for all different conditions. We each made heavy winter moccasins, plus three pairs of sandals. We also tanned hides.

Most of the craftwork was done outside of the BOSS survival school office, which happened to be adjacent to the Anasazi State Park Museum. This provided a nice sideshow for museum visitors, who often sat and watched us after touring the exhibits.

The process of building our primitive-living gear took nearly three months. Though it was enlightening, we became so carried away that rather than building the tools that made the most sense for our location, we built the ones we liked from each different story. Pretty soon, our backpacks weighed fifty pounds each.

Aside from wanting to travel and live like the Native Americans, we were both hoping to reconnect with some of the traditions of the past. We hoped to re-create a trade walk. We brought no cash. Instead, we made trinkets and extra hides to trade for whatever supplies or food we needed.

Our initial destination was Chaco Canyon, which wasn't then but is now a national monument. Historically, Chaco Canyon had been the epicenter for trading in our area. Though we couldn't trade at Chaco, we wanted to see the area, and we knew that there were trading posts run by the Navajo nearby, where we hoped to trade for food and dry goods.

After venturing through Chaco Canyon, we planned to continue across the mountains and canyons. One possibility was ultimately ending up at Winter Count, the annual primitive-skills gathering on the Ak-Chin reservation in Arizona, some four hundred miles and two months away. But any destination was secondary to the feeling we wanted to achieve. We wanted the journey to be something that two men could have embarked on a thousand years ago.

The first steps of the walk felt magical. We were two travelers dressed in long buckskin shirts, breechcloths flapping in the wind, stone knives dangling on the waist, walking down a spring-fed canyon. On our backs were agave fiber packs holding elk skin blankets and buckskin pouches filled with pemmican. Clutched in our hands were bows backed with sinew for added strength, and arrows made of cane tipped with finely honed, razor-sharp chert, a sedimentary rock. Nothing we carried was modern. Everything was handmade from the land and could have been hundreds or even thousands of years old.

I was elated. I felt like we were headed to an ancient city, where people grew corn, beans, squash, and cotton. There, we would trade for what we needed by offering up one of our intricately tanned hides.

Leaving town, we headed straight into the backcountry, through a lush river valley. Within an hour, we were in a place with no people in sight and no hiking trails. But after a couple hours, the practical aspects took hold.

We stopped to take a break to adjust our packs because they were digging into our shoulders. From then on, we had to stop constantly to fiddle with the straps on our backpacks, which seemed to become heavier with each step.

By the end of the day, we were completely worn out from the loads we were carrying. We hadn't done any test walks with the fifty pounds of gear, so we had no idea how taxing it would be. We had forgotten the most basic lesson: be familiar with the load you are carrying.

It was the same thing as the backpacker who buys out the REI store versus the seasoned backpacker who pares down his gear to the bare minimum. Despite the fact that our gear was handmade and paid homage to primitive cultures, carrying so much of it—regardless of how spiritual it might be—was no different from overloading on modern gear. If you haven't used the gear or carried it, there is no way to know how it will perform or how you can perform with it. In short, we had a load of ancient tricks that we didn't fully understand, and we were as uncomfortable as we had ever been in the wilderness.

We stopped for the night to make camp. We were miserable. We built a fire and crawled under our hide skins. The temperature dropped to near zero. In order to preserve our rations, we hadn't eaten the first day. Because we weren't conditioned to go without food, the night was even more uncomfortable.

Intuitively, we knew that food can be hard to come by in the winter months, but at some level we were denying that. We wanted to believe we could walk out onto the landscape and survive off the land at any time. But the reality is that on this landscape everything hunkers down in the winter. This fact was not lost on the native people, who did the same in the winter. The difference was that they spent the fall preparing by stocking up on food.

After the first day, for many reasons, it became evident that the journey would be tougher than we imagined. By the end of the second day, before the sunset, we realized we could not make the trip with the amount of gear we had.

Breck and I discussed what to do. Clearly, we needed to rethink our primitive walk. We decided that in good conscience we couldn't ditch our gear, because we had put so much love into making it. So on the second day, we hiked back to town to drop off our gear and restock with our more technical—and infinitely lighter—gear that we used for teaching outings.

Neither of us felt like we had failed; rather we felt like we had not properly prepared. Back at the BOSS office, we regrouped and repacked. Our packs now held the essentials, such as a knife, a few clay pots, a wool blanket, sandals, wool socks, nylon shorts, and a wool shirt. We exchanged our hide footwear for sandals made from tires.

We also brought a bag of knives and arrowheads we had made, as well as the pemmican. Still, it wasn't like we had gone to the North Face store. Even with a fire burning, sleeping under only a wool blanket on December nights where the temperature hovers around zero still requires a tough constitution physically and mentally to ward off feelings of freezing.

We set back out with our packs at roughly one-third their original weight on what was now a somewhat-primitive walk. We dipped down into the canyon. The changing clouds elevated our spirits. Just before sunset, we discovered a patch of savory oyster mushrooms. It felt like we were on the right path.

That night, a rainstorm rolled in. We found shelter under an overhang in the cliff that gave us protection and lined it with cottonwood leaves. We set up a stone slab just outside the cave and dug a pit to make a fire. We gathered sagebrush bark. Using a fire made from yucca, I spun a coal.

With the fire started, we made a stew of oyster mushrooms, thistle greens, and pemmican. After dinner, we sat in the cave in silence, writing in our journals. The temperature hovered around twenty-five degrees, but the cave was so toasty warm that we were both in shorts.

But as we began to look ahead, it became apparent that we were seeing different things. We were camped in an area where we had guided, and therefore knew the terrain well. Soon we would be miles away, in a new land. I had the mind of an explorer. I was anxious to experience the land like a newborn baby, seeing, feeling, hearing, and smelling life for the first time.

Breck, however, was in a different mental space. As hard as we had prepared for the trip, we had never addressed the emotional aspect. He was thinking of his girlfriend, whom he had been dating for a year. Ahead for him was the time they would be apart.

Over the next few days, it was clear that his focus was wandering. We talked on and off about what he was going through. His emotions were pulling him back to his normal life, even as he needed them to be wholly invested in the journey.

Tensions between us began to rise. Admittedly, I wasn't offering any comforting words. I didn't have the personality or experience to empathize with what he was going through, because I hadn't put any energy into a long-term relationship at that point in my life. There was no way I could motivate him to finish the journey and then deal with his emotions. As much promise as the journey held, it was also going to be very tough physically and mentally. If one person was slightly off, it would eventually break the other.

We both realized we were processing different thoughts and needed time with those thoughts. So at the end of the first week, without any acrimony, we split up. Breck turned back. I pressed on.

I watched him split off in the distance, as we both climbed out of the canyon. He traveled in a northwest direction to get up on the rim of the canyon, and I headed straight north.

It began to snow the day we parted. The first major winter storm was approaching, and the animals were preparing their homes and storing food. The wind was cold, but the scenery was spectacular. I was surrounded by snowcapped mesas topped with clouds that looked like whipped cream. Above the clouds was a searing blue sky. The snow was not only beautiful but also gave me moisture for the hike.

Once Breck and I had shed our all-primitive gear, the journey had lost its purity. We had started out with a very specific goal in mind. We had painted a clear picture in our minds and for others. We had told everyone we were going out in primitive gear, that we were going to re-create a trade route, and that we were going to collect salt along the way. We were going to trade tools and goods like our primitive ancestors did. We had set a certain expectation, rather than keeping our goal vague and doing it for the sake of exploration and for ourselves.

But now that we had parted, I was still on a journey. Even though I no longer felt a calling to go to Chaco Canyon or to the Navajo trading post, I needed to consider my circumstances in no less a way than the indigenous people of the area would have done. I was entering a potentially dangerous survival situation.

The fact is, the Boulder area is a pretty hard environment to live in during the wintertime without a house or regular access to a grocery store. I knew that I hadn't gathered enough food to make it through the winter. I also didn't have that much money at the time. It wasn't like I could check out of my lifestyle, rent a place, and buy some food. But aside from not having the financial means, I didn't have the desire to do that.

I figured that as a follower of primitive-living skills, my best alternative was to migrate south. That meant walking until I reached lower elevations, where there would be more natural resources. At the same time, I established a second goal: to walk the four hundred miles to Winter Count, the annual primitive-skills gathering in Arizona. In reality, because of all the zigzags, my walk would be closer to six hundred miles.

As I thought about what had been lost, I began to feel that more could be gained by walking to Winter Count. The goal that Breck and I had set was to go through Chaco Canyon to *feel* what it had been like back when twenty thousand Native Americans traded goods there. But the fact is, Chaco Canyon was now a national monument where people came to see the ruins, not trade goods.

Winter Count, however, was a real gathering of 450 like-minded people. All my friends would be there. In essence, it was our Chaco Canyon. We met there to trade goods, as well as lessons and stories. It would be a similar experience, only now I was actually chasing something real rather than an ideal that had disappeared long ago.

After Breck and I parted, I walked through an area called Little Egypt, which is known for its resemblance to the rolling sand dunes of the Middle Eastern country. It was surreal to be walking across sand dunes that were being carpeted with a thin layer of snow.

After I topped out of the canyon, I ended up on the Kaiparowits Plateau. Snow began falling more heavily, accumulating to about six inches. It was a peaceful snow, not the kind that drifts. There was very little wind. I was wearing sandals with no socks, but the snow was so powdery that as long as I kept moving, I was able to stay warm. The canyon had numerous caves in its walls, which provided a sense of security should the snow pick up.

As the sun began to set, I looked for shelter for the night. I found a rock overhang and I hunkered down. I built a reflector wall and then made a fire. The fire was built outside the cave, up against the reflector wall rock, facing toward me in the cave. This allows the smoke to escape and the heat to be contained, but also does not tarnish the cave wall as making a fire inside the cave would.

Once the fire was lit, I crawled into that space. I felt a sense of peace and joy. I sat in the rock ledge, watching the snowfall. I was warm and cozy in a cocoon of rock, with the heat from the fire, and I had put it up in a matter of minutes.

The truth is, that shelter can be put up faster than most backpackers could set up their tent and camp. Even in a tent, most people would be uncomfortable with such low temperatures and snow. The reflector rock made all the difference. It is set up outside the cave, and the fire is then built on the inside of the wall. The wall contains the heat in the cave and can easily add twenty to thirty degrees of warmth to the space.

The evening was made even more blissful now that I had restored purpose to my journey.

EPIC SURVIVAL RULE #4:

DEAL WITH DANGER

In the wild, the demands are immediate and constant, and I am the only one who can guard myself against the danger.

Sure, cities are full of dangers, but much of modern society is consumed by guarding against these dangers. People protect themselves with everything from proper shoes to safer cars to door locks for their homes. Houses are insulated against cold, and air-conditioning and heat provide comfort and safety.

When these people venture out into the wild, they strive to reach the point where they feel at one with nature. They go backpacking or hiking because they want to leave their houses. Yet most go on a shopping spree at the REI store and stuff their backpacks full of gear because they are so afraid that if they don't have these things, they will not be able to survive.

I also often hear about people in the wild being scared of the animals. Dealing with wild animals is rooted in respecting them and their environment. They sense someone who respects their land.

Once I was in the backcountry and a mountain lion spotted me. It just stopped and stared. Then it began moving its head rhythmically from side to side, like a Michael Jackson maneuver in slow motion. It kept staring intently into my eyes. At that point, I felt like there was a soul exchange, that we were both reading each other. That mountain lion was like a brother, if you will, and it felt as though we had a mutual understanding that he wouldn't hurt me if I didn't hurt his land.

The demands of the wild can be unpredictable and sometimes life threatening, but I am finding that dangerous situations can be handled in different ways. I try to avoid putting myself in danger, but that is not always possible.

Chapter Thirteen

GOING IT ALONE

The Kaiparowits Plateau is massive and intimidating. Once home to the ancient Paiute people, the area stretches for forty miles and has varying terrain. There are extensive flat clay surfaces, narrow canyons, and several undulating ranges. I was entering it in what would be my first winter with no home other than the untainted landscape, which made my spirit soar and allowed me to feel like I was living in a long-lost culture. I had four hundred miles to go to reach the Winter Count gathering in Page, Arizona, and much to discover.

After walking for two days along the Kaiparowits Plateau, I got down to the flats. There were no trees. The bushes grew only about six inches tall. There was nothing for me to keep a fire going. I was tired so I just sat down on the barren flatwash, scanning the horizon for shelter. The temperatures were dropping severely. It was going to be one of my coldest nights ever in the wilderness—and I had no shelter.

I started to have doubts about my skills. I felt like I was in the wrong place at the wrong time—a potentially deadly mixture when you are alone in the wilderness. I was frustrated that I wasn't farther south. I was even more upset that I hadn't made it to a proper shelter for the night. I also realized there was no way I could use the fire-starting techniques I had used in the cave, because there was no fuel to burn.

I had a sense that I should get up and keep going. I knew I was near a highway. I thought, *Maybe I should just call this journey good, run out to the highway tonight, put my thumb out, and end in Page, where I could have a hot meal and a warm bed.*

As it was getting dark, with less than a half hour of daylight remaining, I sat back and scanned the wash. Rather than continuing down a path of self-doubt, I began to use my powers of observation.

Not far, maybe a quarter mile away, I noticed that there was a little bit of a pocket in a rock. It wasn't big enough to be a cave. What was it?

I went over to investigate. The pocket was about five feet long—not long enough to stretch out in, but long enough to curl up for the night. Shelter.

I couldn't start a fire, so I began to explore options the land could provide for warmth. Nearby, I spotted six-inch-tall rabbit brush growing wild. A big wash cut through the brush. I looked more closely. The roots were being eroded by the wash, and the rabbit brush was actually falling.

I walked through the wash and started pulling the loose rabbit brush. The base was twiggy, and the ends were feathery. It would make ideal bedding. I gathered the rabbit brush in bundles and stuffed the rock pocket with it. Then I burrowed out an area and crawled inside. The shell of rock was completely insulated by rabbit brush. I slept very well that night, as the land had granted me just enough to give me the courage to continue.

The next morning, I woke up fairly early. I continued walking toward the dam that stretches across the Colorado River that would take me toward Page, Arizona. From there, I walked another ten miles to Page.

Just as I was coming off the Kaiparowits, a ranger stopped me. He asked where I was going. I gave him the best description of my route that I could. I told him I was going to follow the Colorado River and then try to find a way into the Grand Canyon, which was a hundred miles away from where we were. When he heard the words *Grand Canyon*, it sparked his authority. He told me I would need a permit to enter the Grand Canyon. I explained to him that I was doing a walkabout on a whim, and that I hadn't planned to stop at a ranger station. The ranger insisted I needed a permit. I appealed to him that I had once done trail work in the Grand Canyon for five months, and added that I didn't have the financial means to buy a permit.

But he couldn't be swayed. He told me that I would have to go to the Paria ranger station. Because Jesse Perry and I had been to the area on our walkabout, I knew the station was at least ten miles out of the way, meaning twenty miles round-trip. I nodded and gave him the "sure, whatever" treatment.

I continued into town to the Navajo trading post. I had a few things I didn't need, and I wanted to add one more layer of warmth. I ended up trading a pair of moccasins and a stone knife for two thin wool blankets. I now had those two blankets, plus the wool one I had brought. The idea was that I could ditch my pack basket and roll my gear in a blanket. I would have to rely on my tire sandals for the rest of the journey. Though I knew I would have to walk through snow, my feet hadn't been cold. I was more concerned about warmth at night, though as it turns out, the human obstacles were going to give me greater troubles. The trade was the type of calculated risk I often have to make.

After I left the trading post, I headed off the highway, away from the roads. I ended up in a maze of slot canyons. A slot canyon is a tight, narrow canyon where you can often touch both sides by extending your arms. The walls range from ten to three hundred feet in height and can prevent you from seeing what lies ahead. It was very confusing terrain, but I knew that if I could navigate the canyons, then the route would take me over Echo Cliffs.

Moving from the southeast over the top and going to the northwest side, I continued another thirty-plus miles and walked over Echo Cliffs and into Marble Canyon. A hole-in-the-wall place, Marble Canyon has a hotel and a gift shop but not much else. (The Marble Canyon Lodge is where I had met Jesse when he returned to our journey.)

Just as I was about to cross Highway 89 into the Navajo reservation, the same ranger drove up in his truck and motioned me over.

The country was wide open. With a pair of powerful binoculars, you can see for miles. Clearly, the ranger had been tracking me.

The ranger asked me if I had gotten my permit. I told him there was no place on my route where I could get one. He then informed me that I would have to go to the Lees Ferry ranger station, which was eight miles out of the way, or sixteen miles round-trip.

I tried to explain my situation. I told him that I was exhausted. I was crossing some 120 miles alone with mostly primitive gear. My respect for the land was absolute. After all, I had only a small roll of supplies, on which I was traveling hundreds of miles. I appealed to him to let me continue my journey without any bureaucratic interference.

But he wouldn't budge. And he didn't offer me a ride, either—not that I would have taken it.

In nature, I teach my students to think for themselves. Rules, I tell them, are a guideline. To me, that incident showed that this ranger was not thinking for himself. He could plainly see that I had no money and that I respected the land. He knew my story was legitimate; yet he was not willing to let me go.

There was another dynamic at work. I walked everywhere in my life.

The result was that some days I looked good, while other days I was really dirty and looked tired and hungry. Authority figures often assumed I was a homeless bum, and they would harass me in different ways. It was ironic. People who are supposed to be protectors harassed me. It left me with a bitter feeling toward authority. It was also frustrating because I was trying to lead a humble existence and be a steward of the earth, yet people who likely were not living as respectfully tried to defile my existence.

I had no choice. I walked in the direction of the ranger station. I decided that the fastest way was to run it both ways. I stashed my pack in the woods and ran the eight miles to the ranger station.

When I arrived, the situation turned into a fiasco. First, the ranger on duty insisted that I call the ranger station in the Grand Canyon, where I was headed. The ranger on the phone asked me where I planned to camp every night. Being honest, I said I didn't have a clue. The Grand Canyon ranger asked my route. I told him I had seen a place to enter the Grand Canyon near the Little Colorado, and I asked if I could get in there. He wasn't sure; no one had ever been over there.

I explained that I used to work in the park and asked him to waive the fee given my history with the area. The ranger seemed sympathetic, but said he could not go against "regulations." The permit was $55.

To put things into perspective, I had about $350 to my name. For most people, paying $55 would not be a big deal, but it literally cost me one-seventh of my money. Federal park officials don't realize that there are people who live in the bush full-time, and when they are forced to cough up those fees, it can be a significant chunk of their wealth. That ranger had no comprehension of what that meant. That was why I was upset with the process.

When I asked the ranger what the money was used for, he told me it was for "the knowledge and resources we supply to the public." So I turned that around on him and told him that if he would waive the fee, I would let the ranger station know if the route was doable. He gave me the whole "dude, man" speech.

"Believe me, I totally get it, man," he said. "I understand what you are doing. If it were up to me, dude, I'd pay you for that. But I've got my boss listening over my shoulder."

I stopped him. "I'll just do the route and let you know if it's viable; then you will have information to give up to others," I said. "It's on me."

I felt I was due a favor, particularly if I discovered a route they had never traveled—not possibly couldn't travel.

I paid the money that I really could not afford to spend, and ran back to retrieve my sack. I then trekked thirty miles across the Navajo reservation and came to the entry point for the route I had asked him about, which dropped into the Little Colorado valley. I studied the gazetteer map that I had torn from an old book, but it wasn't very helpful. It was not like a regular topo map, where you can see the trails and details of the land features.

Just as I was about to head down, I encountered a Navajo man. I was standing at a fork in the trail. I asked him if I could get down into the canyon.

The man smiled. "Oh sure," he said, gesturing in no particular direction.

"Sorry . . . right or left?" I asked.

"Just dat-a-way," he said. Then he turned and walked away.

So I was left to my own devices to choose. I guessed right. Soon I ran into a sheer cliff. Just below it was a trail the Navajo had built to get down to the bottom of the canyon.

It was a steep, switchbacky trail, but it seemed purposefully carved out. When I reached the bottom, I discovered the purpose for the trail. The Navajo had built a fishing camp at the very bottom, some two thousand–plus feet below the cliff. As there were nets strung across the river, I knew the fishing camp was still active.

No one was there. I looked around. There was no evidence of anyone having been there recently, probably for at least a month. But the camp was still intact.

I didn't invest the energy into fishing there, because I couldn't physically see any fish. The water was turquoise, but I could see only a foot down into it. I didn't have any fishing supplies. Even though I was skilled at catching fish with my hands, without being able to see them, that wasn't an option.

In fact, the only food I was getting was trapped mice and rats. I would stop every night and make traps. That was my skill level at that point. I was carrying a bow and arrow, but I wasn't a skilled hunter by any means. Part of the journey for me was to develop those skills. So I was living off that little bit of meat and a few rations, such as pinole, that I had brought.

The country was very dry and barren. From the vague map I had, I determined that I would have about forty miles of dangerously dry travel. I was walking through a very shallow canyon that was about thirty feet deep and cut through the clay beds, which made me conscious that I needed to be aware of my water sources.

After several miles, I found a pocket of water containing a few gallons. Water had gathered in a depression in the rock from rain and also from meltwater that had flowed down from higher elevations. There was a cave next to it. I sat in the cave and hydrated.

I began to carefully consider how much farther I had to go without the ability to carry water. Given the heat and the lack of any consistent water, the journey would be a rough one. Instead of moving on, I decided to use my ability to be patient. Though I was avoiding a survival situation, I was also putting myself in one. But my experience was telling me that staying was less risky than moving.

I needed to listen to the land. I had to have the patience to stop and wait for the land to tell me when it was time to move. That was a hugely valuable—and intuitively difficult to grasp—tool. Generally, only a hunter-gatherer has the patience and ability to execute this strategy. Basically, I was risking starving to death, because I felt my heightened relationship with the land would deliver me what I needed to survive.

This was a major step for me. The impatience of youth was being conquered. The inaction I was taking was the polar opposite of what the kid who ran everywhere would have done. He would not have been able to sit in a cave for an undetermined number of days and wait for rain. But I could.

There was an inherent risk. Every hour I sat in the cave, the water supply in front of me dwindled, as I drank it and watched it seep into the ground and evaporate into the dry air. When I first hunkered down in the cave, there was no sign of weather, no clouds or noticeable dew in the air.

I had water for the time being, but not much food. I had cornmeal to make ash cakes, which are cooked directly over the heat of a fire. With cornmeal, I cook it on a rock at a forty-five-degree angle until it hardens, and then I finish cooking it directly on the hot ash. I used the leftover corn niblets to trap mice. I ate mice every day. Though I was consuming less than five hundred calories a day, it was enough to sustain me. Despite the lack of food, I was much more concerned about getting enough hydration to make the forty-mile crossing through the barren flats of the Navajo reservation.

The landscape was relatively flat. The reddish clay surface was intermixed with shallow washes of sandstone. Those washes were where I would get water after it rained. Actually, the moisture that fell in the area was more a slushy half-rain, half-snow mixture. The temperatures were reasonable, fifty degrees in the day and around thirty degrees at night, but once the sun rose, any of that slushy mixture that fell into the wash would melt fairly quickly.

The issue was that the deepest washes were no more than a couple inches. In harder stone, there would be slick rock pools as deep as ten feet. These can hold water for two months, whereas the small pools dry up in a matter of hours. Immediately after a slushy rain, the small pools would hold water just long enough for me to move across the land.

While waiting for rain, I stayed in the cave all day. I worked on a few crafts and condensed my load. But for the most part, I sat and meditated. After a day and a half of being in the cave, I started seeing a little cloud buildup. It wasn't dense enough to release any moisture, but I felt that it would in another day or so.

I had been living with the land so much that at home in Utah I was actually able to predict the weather. As incredible as that sounds, I could tell people weeks in advance when it would rain, how many days it was going to rain, and how hard. I hoped I had connected with the Arizona land closely enough that my premonitions of rain would be correct.

On my third night in the cave, the clouds opened up and dumped a significant amount of rain on the land. It rained hard, filling the pockets with water. I set out the next morning. The rain allowed me to stay hydrated as I traversed the thirty-plus miles across the flats.

I followed the Little Colorado River down into the Grand Canyon. The river is magical in the wintertime because the water is still a comfortable seventy-five degrees. I passed an old salt mine and grabbed some salt for the journey. I knew that a white man wasn't supposed to take salt, but in many ways I felt closer to the Navajo and Hopi so I took a small amount and continued on my journey.

By the time I reached the Grand Canyon, I was pretty spent. I had no reserves. I was cold. I didn't know it, but I would soon be in grave danger.

Chapter Fourteen

A CLOSE ENCOUNTER
WITH DEATH

The winter solstice in the Grand Canyon changes everything. The grandeur of nature's remarkable creation dims. When the sun is at its lowest point on the horizon and shines the least amount of hours, you cannot see it at the bottom of the canyon. The day is in constant shade. When the light fades, it drags the temperature down with it.

Because I had lived in the area years earlier, by the time I was several thousand feet down in the canyon, I had an idea where I was. My original plan was to stay in the bottom and hike along the Colorado River and then pop out. However, with the low temperatures and lack of sun, I knew that wasn't a viable option.

My entire body was beaten. I was cold and hungry. I was wearing a very thin wool shirt with no pockets and a pair of nylon shorts. I had to get into the sunlight. Rather than cross the canyon, I decided to climb out.

I climbed up toward the rim, thinking that at the very least I would be exposed to some sunshine. My idea was to eventually hike to the South Rim and resupply some food staples. That would have been twenty-five miles. I had traversed more than two hundred miles, weaving my way through deserts and canyons, from Utah into Northern Arizona, so this seemed very doable.

As I was hiking up, it started snowing. Within an hour, the snow was coming down in sheets. I was wearing sandals, as I had traded away my lined moccasins for an extra blanket. I had known the trade was a risk, but I thought I would be farther south when the heavy snow came. I had no socks. I was generating heat by moving, but my body temperature had dropped slightly, so I did not have much heat to give. The snow was falling so rapidly that it rose somewhere between my mid-calf and knee. The wind was also picking up, limiting my vision. The visibility was so bad that I couldn't tell I was in the Grand Canyon.

It was getting later in the day and colder with each step. I needed to warm up my feet. I left the trail and undid my bundle. I unrolled one of the thin blankets, cut off the bottom, and then cut it into two big squares. I removed my sandals and wrapped my feet in those two squares of wool, and I then tied my sandals back on.

The realization hit me that I was going to die dressed in a thin wool shirt and nylon shorts. I took the saddle blanket I had brought and cut a slit in the middle. I threw it over my head and tied it around my waist like a poncho. I was in such a dire survival situation that I was cutting up my blankets. This would render them useless later, but there wouldn't be a later if I didn't make it out of here.

I continued pistoling toward the top. I reached the top right at dusk. The sun had gone down, and it was getting dark fast. With every step, I sank into the snow. My legs were numb from the cold.

I finally stopped. I couldn't go any farther. My thoughts turned to surviving. If I could make it through the night, I could reach sunlight in the morning. I looked around to see if I could find some insulation for shelter. It was no use; everything was blanketed in two feet of snow.

I needed to get a fire going. Without a fire starter, I would have to spin a coal. I looked at my hands and started to move them. I could feel the onset of hypothermia. I tested my hands by rapidly opening and closing them. My fingers barely moved. I was telling my fingers to move, but they wouldn't. They were too cold to spin up the fire.

I had reached my outer limit of exhaustion. I was out of food and energy. Many times I had pushed my body in terms of lack of calories and against the cold, but I was aware that I had gone too far.

I stood there in the blowing snow. There was no dry place to lie down. I knew that if I lay down in the snow, I would freeze to death and die in the night. The nearest village was still at least fifteen miles away.

Though it was the middle of the night and too overcast for the moon to light my way, I decided my best chance to live was to try to walk the fifteen miles. With my physical gifts and my mind's ability to focus, I believed I could plow through the snowdrifts and make it to safety.

I could feel frostbite on my nose and cheeks. I tucked my face into my makeshift coat to try and warm my skin and ward off permanent damage. My body was completely defeated because I didn't have the caloric resources to maintain warmth. My core temperature was barely on the functional side. I could feel hypothermia setting in, as my joints tightened and my pulse slowed.

I continued walking directly into the wind. A hard, sharp, icy snow was slashing my face. I was freezing. I didn't have the energy to shiver. I was beyond that stage and I was not really conscious of what was going on. The functions of my body felt like they were slowing down.

Moving was my last-ditch effort to stay warm. I don't know how I was moving. My body had never been that far gone. Several times I collapsed in the snow. On one fall, I hit hard and ended up on my back. I lay there for a while, not fully conscious.

I summoned the energy to get to my feet. I walked another few steps. But eventually, no more. I fell down. The lights in my brain went out.

Time passed. I woke up and came to the realization that I was lying in the snow, unable to move. I looked up and saw lily-white flakes falling from nature's ceiling into my eyes. Even in my depleted state, I appreciated their elegance. I said to myself, "Thank you, God, I had a great life. I really appreciate it."

I was certain I was going to die; yet I was okay with it. It was time to go do something else. I closed my eyes.

Then I heard a voice. "Your mom's gonna be pissed if you die in the snow," it said. "She'll be forever cursing your primitive skills and earth-living life if you die here."

I couldn't place the voice, but it didn't matter. I wouldn't call it motivation because I certainly did not want to die, but upon hearing the voice, I slowly rose to my feet. Putting what mattered over mind, not trying to muscle my way but just attempting to move, I continued both my trek to town and my life, which, at that point, were intertwined.

I later found out that it was minus eight degrees with a wind chill of at least twenty degrees below zero. Even for the Grand Canyon on the shortest day of the year, the conditions were particularly dire.

How did I find the energy to get up and walk when I seemingly had none?

I learned that it was a classic boost of adrenaline triggered by fear that can occur when the body is challenged to its limits. Likely, my body temperature had dropped below the danger level of ninety and was nearing eighty-two, the trip line for loss of consciousness. In a study, Vladimir Zatsiorsky, a professor of kinesiology at Penn State and an expert in the biomechanics of weight lifting, found that an ordinary person can summon 65 percent of their strength in normal circumstances, whereas a weight lifter can summon 85 percent. In competition, a trained athlete can go 12 percent above those figures. But with an adrenaline surge, the short-term push can be double those figures.

As Dr. Sam Parnia explains, under extreme stress, the adrenal gland dumps adrenaline into the bloodstream, blood pressure surges, and the heart pushes oxygen to the muscles. "Performance is multiplied, and every fiber and muscle in your body functions a hundred times better," Dr. Parnia says. "You become superhuman for a short period of time. For Matt, because he is so fit and can deliver oxygen at a much higher level, his adrenaline surge would be even more extreme."

I also attributed surviving to my ability to deal with fear. I had reached the brink. I knew what it would feel like to die. Fear was present, but it did not consume me; therefore I did not succumb to it. Fear can lock people up and prevent them from thinking clearly. It can debilitate the mind and the body. However, people who have the ability to relax have faster reflexes; whereas more fear translates to slower reflexes, as a doctor once told me.

Coping with fear requires calm. In my experience in the wild, anytime fear creeps up, I try to relax into it rather than allow it to consume me. If you tense up, everything about you starts to fall apart. Climbing initially taught me how to deal with fear. It was get up the rock or die. That type of fear showed in my clunky technique. But once I learned to respect the rock and be in touch with my movements, awareness trumped fear.

Lack of fear also brings clarity. I was lying in the snow, hours from freezing to death. My skills and judgment were being questioned. The result of not answering would be final. But I inherently knew I had a connection to the environment that had taken me down.

I did not feel that I was being reckless. I was not attempting to challenge the land out of hubris. I was not trying to prove anything to anyone, or find anything. I am not a pioneer, nor am I an explorer. I was a person living the way millions of people over hundreds of thousands of year have lived. The wall I found myself up against was a circumstance of my life.

I have always believed that in the wild if you're open and honest with your environment, there will be a connection—you take care of it and it takes care of you. If everything you do has an honesty and integrity to it, even if you are in a difficult situation, you won't feel a high degree of fear. If you look at the big picture—I'm alone in the wilderness, stuck in subfreezing conditions with no communication—you will be uncomfortable. But if you can step back and isolate that one spot where you are and focus on it, you won't be afraid of the unseen and unknown. For me, those were the skills I had devoted my life to pursuing.

The adrenaline surge likely gave me energy to push on, and my ability to focus on where I was allowed me to use that productively—not that the rest of the trip was easy by any means.

I eventually reached the south village. Unfortunately, I was on the east side, which I soon found out was closed for the winter. My immediate thought was that I would die if I didn't get inside a warm building. I planned to use what little bit of cash I had and check into a hotel. But when I reached the hotel, it had a sign that informed me it was closed for the season.

I looked around. There were two feet of snow on the ground and no signs of any life at all.

I said to myself out loud, "I can't make it another two miles to the next village." That actually made me smile, because in all the time I spent alone, I had probably not uttered more than two or three sentences out loud.

I was spent. I had barely made it to the doorstep of that hotel. My first thought was to find shelter somewhere, anywhere. I was freezing, so I needed more than just a dry spot. Perhaps there was a doorway, or even a garbage Dumpster. I looked around. The buildings were square, brick box structures. I didn't see any doorways or awnings.

I started walking back out into the road area. It was covered with snow. But I noticed that there was one set of tire tracks. Though they were filling with snow, they made walking a little easier. It also gave me hope that someone might drive through.

I felt like I wasn't going to make it. I didn't know what to do. I walked a few hundred yards, and then I saw my salvation. A white van with heavy chains clanking hard on the road was coming right at me.

Given how I looked, I thought there was no way they were going to give some crazy-looking mountain man a ride. I thought about lying down in the middle of the road, but quickly reconsidered. I put out my thumb.

The van stopped. The driver, a man bundled up, pushed the door open from the inside and offered me a ride. I pulled myself in and thanked him.

It turned out that he worked for the town and was picking up employees who were out drinking late at night. Where, I had no idea, because the place looked deserted.

He dropped me at the nearest hotel. The desk clerk didn't seem all that shocked at my appearance. I checked in and went to my room.

I unrolled my pack and spread out the contents to allow the warm air to dry them. I went into the bathroom and ran my hands under lukewarm water. When I looked in the mirror, I realized my face had some minor frostbite on my cheeks and nose, but I would be okay. I took a warm bath, dried myself, and then crawled into bed. I fell asleep immediately. What happened next was majestic.

Chapter Fifteen

VISIONS AND VISION QUESTS

In life, time carries youth forward, and young men and women become adults. While there are traditional and nontraditional paths to maturity, the first rite of passage in life is often when people leave home. Leaving home, be it for college, military service, or any other reason is the first step into adulthood. That separation carries with it a sense of heading off alone to stake your own claim. Even in the cocoon of a university, surrounded by friends and supported by parents, young adults experience independence, and begin to search for their path forward. In the Native American cultures, they would escalate this experience by going on a vision quest, which I have found can be a powerful survival tool.

Native Americans have a connection with the land that is absolute. Many of their traditions and ceremonies have become precedents for the modern customs that people use to better their spiritual lives. Some of the Native American tools for growth, such as the vision quest, have not translated to modern society, though in this case many people would greatly benefit if it did. Vision quests are a way for the Native Americans to advance their lives. As a survivalist, they have moved me forward both spiritually and emotionally.

A typical Native American vision quest lasts four days and four nights. (Going out into the wilderness for two full nights and one full day can also yield benefits.) It takes place in a location with only the most minimal of possessions. Typically, a stone circle is constructed and the person does not leave the area. The vision quest includes four stages: solitude, immersion in nature, fasting, and community. Being alone forces one to look inside his own soul. The return to nature creates connection. Fasting opens the body up to absorb possibilities. The return to community with this newfound elixir helps others.

Most vision quests are purposeful and forced. Native Americans go on them to find their spiritual center, to reinvent themselves, and to chart their life's direction. They use them to guide themselves in many pursuits, to open cathartic doors, and to recover from life-altering events. Once the body has opened itself up to nature, the mind has an ability to see it in an unconfined way. In other words, you can't sit in your apartment, turn off the TV, and have this experience.

Vision quests are part of the fabric of nature and owe their power to the natural world. Being alone in nature causes the body to go into a more relaxed state. When the body reaches that state, it becomes more receptive. On these quests, the person often experiences visions because their mind becomes comatose from lack of food and sleep.

Starving yourself depletes your energy. When you have a normal level of energy, you are an "outputter." The body constantly wants to push that energy somewhere. The idea on a vision quest is that you reach a point where you have no energy to push out anymore. So instead of pushing out energy, the body receives energy from other aspects around it, primarily the land and other spiritual sources.

I have talked to people who have studied aspects of people's energy. Some people are born with more of their own energy, while others are born as empty vessels. People born as empty vessels usually have greater intuition and psychic abilities, and they are able to receive things. Some people have energy but lack a highly developed knowing center (the center of wisdom people are born with).

To break it down, there are energy channels that run through your mind, body, and spirit. Some people are always receiving that energy; they are not putting any out. These would typically be shamans. They would also be people who would be able to sit on a vision quest and find a profound spiritual revelation.

According to spiritual readers who have read me, I am less of a receiver than most. When I sit on a vision quest, I don't see the proverbial white buffalo. One aspect about me that is unique is that all my energy centers are fully developed, along with my knowing center. That means I have the ability to be a teacher and to share the knowledge I was born with.

The land will share with anyone who puts themselves into the state of receiver. Most people who go through the first three stages will have some form of vision. Native Americans believe that people who need it the most receive it far more frequently. Therefore, if somebody who is already well grounded walks into the vision circle for four days and four nights and doesn't have some powerful vision, the shaman's explanation would be that you were grounded enough in that moment that you did not need to see anything big.

I have used vision quests whenever I need clarity. Upon moving to Boulder, before I applied for the job at BOSS, I went to the top of a mesa to see what the land had to tell me. I spent three days and three nights (the typical time for a vision quest) in a circle there to connect with the land where I would work and I found my home. But I have also experienced powerful visions while out in nature that have helped me survive.

My journey on the "revised" all-primitive walk that led me into the Grand Canyon was similar to a vision quest. Like the Native American men on a vision quest, I was experiencing extreme solitude. I was purely connected to the land. My body was beaten down. I was nearly starving. When I arrived at the motel, I was not consciously seeking anything. Even though I was hungry, food wasn't on my mind. All I wanted was a hot bath to raise my core body temperature to a reasonable level and a warm bed for a night's sleep.

I crawled under the sheets and pulled up the covers. I was focused on nothing. There were flashes of my near-death experience. I wasn't planning for tomorrow. I didn't even say a prayer of thanks for my life being spared. I went right to sleep.

I have always been a lucid dreamer and a light sleeper. I owe that to living in the wilderness. Even during sleep, there has to be a level of awareness because there are so many variables. As I developed the ability to detect danger in sleep, I also found that I could easily recall my dreams and separate them from reality.

That night, I began dreaming before I fell into a deep sleep. I was aware of the precise moment when my dream started to take shape. I liken it to the feeling when you start dozing off and fuzzily enter a dream state before fully checking out. This dream started the instant I pressed my head into the pillow—the first pillow that had been under my head in a couple years.

I saw my spot, my place in life, my oasis. It was something of a wilderness area that didn't have a lot of distinctive features to it. The ground was covered with sand and a few trees dotted the land, but it was a very nondescript place. As I prepared to walk toward that spot, a man riding on what appeared to be a hovercraft approached me from the distance. The vehicle had no wheels and was elevated two to three feet off the ground like something out of the movie *Back to the Future Part II*. By the time the vehicle reached me, my sleep was getting deeper and deeper.

The hovercraftlike vehicle stopped in front of me. The man was of a tan Caucasian ancestry and held his face with a certain amount of compassion and wisdom, much like the actor Morgan Freeman would if he were playing the role.

"Hop in," the man said.

Puzzled, I replied, "Where are we going?"

"I'm taking you to your house," he said casually, as if he were giving a friend a lift home. "Your wife is there waiting for you."

"House? Wife? I'm not married," I said.

His demeanor turned stern. "Matt," he said. "You have dedicated your whole life to teaching primitive skills and teaching people how to live with the earth. This is what's been waiting for you." He punched the phrase *whole life*, though I wasn't sure what that meant.

I hopped on, and off we went. I was an adventurer on his strangest adventure ever. A mysterious excitement took hold.

The drive wasn't long. We pulled up to a house. It was the most beautiful structure I could conceptualize. The house had a white-picket-fence feel without actually having a white picket fence. The awning and entrance to the door were formed from a log that created a natural upside-down U shape. All the materials were of the earth, but the house had been built with a human mind for detail.

Just as I stepped off the hover car, the front door opened. An absolutely gorgeous woman walked out. She was dressed simply, which accentuated her natural beauty. There seemed to be a celestial light radiating from her. She walked up to me.

"Don't you think it's kind of strange that we are married and we don't really know each other?" I managed.

The corners of her mouth turned up as she spoke. "But I do know you and you know me," she said reassuringly.

Instantly, I understood what she meant. My fuzzy thoughts became clear. We walked into the house and back into our lives together. From that point forward, there were no words in the dream.

We spent an entire week together getting to know each other again and making the house our own. I worked on the physical tasks, while she took care of the more graceful pursuits. For instance, I would build a table out of wood, and she would make a flower centerpiece. Everything we did had a synchronicity to it that didn't require us to ask the other what to do. Our roles seemed perfectly defined. We were blissfully intertwined.

Six hours after the man picked me up, I awoke. I felt enlightened. The dream had taken up the entire six hours. Many experts claim that the longest dreams only last up to twenty minutes and occur only during REM sleep, but this was not the case. I know this because I recalled the precise moment the dream began, just as I crossed from consciousness to sleep.

The dream I had was unique, and I knew it. It was born of the harrowing experience I had in the Grand Canyon. Unlike a vision quest, I had not been seeking answers to my path forward. I have been on full vision quests for four days and four nights and not had such clear visions as I did in that dream. Still, I could not ascribe any larger meaning to it at that time.

My most complete visions have come on hunter-gatherer-type walkabouts in which I am living off the land for long periods of time. Most of the time I'm alone, but sometimes I'm guiding groups. Sometimes when I guide on long courses for a couple weeks, students will have visions that make me jealous. In part, this is because the previously uninitiated body is more receptive once it is put in a state where it can be an "inputter," rather than "outputter."

These visions tend to be highly stylized versions of something missing from their lives. Perhaps their late father said something so profound that it wouldn't be in an ordinary dream. Recalling such visions, the people are often in tears because they feel they have been touched by something real and lasting.

When students go through the starvation phase, they often start dreaming that they were with friends feasting at a banquet. Some people wake up and brush it off, saying it was merely a dream. But if the dream endures, others like myself enjoy the experience so much that when we wake up, even though we know it was a dream or a vision, we feel like we actually ate the feast and hung out with friends.

Like many people, in my early days I may have discounted such an experience, dismissing it as an ordinary dream or a hallucination, from being too hot and too dehydrated. But I have had visions that show these accounts are more than mere dreams or the side effects of a depleted body, and that things are connected more deeply.

I began to understand this on a long walkabout. I ended up staying out in the canyons alone for forty-two days. After about eight days, I found a cave in which to rest. I didn't sit in the cave as a substitute for a vision quest circle. Instead, I decided to purify my body by drinking mint tea and not eating any other food.

I stayed in the cave for a week. I was wearing a breechcloth and had another piece of cloth tied around my waist. Those were my only belongings. My primary daily activities consisted of leaving to collect mint and water from a spring that was deeply cut into the ravine below, and building a fire at night. I did little else.

On the fourth night, I was lying on the cloth by the fire preparing to go to sleep. My skin was exposed to the night sky and the fire. Seconds after I fell asleep, I heard a noise coming from the spring down the hill. I woke up.

I sat up and looked at the fire. The smoldering flames looked real, but I realized I hadn't woken up my real body because I could still feel the fire on my shoulder. It was a variation of my body, my consciousness, in a place that was identical to where I had fallen asleep.

I was puzzled. I didn't know how to react to this feeling. I was listening to the spring and looking down the hill, all the while wondering what I might be looking for. The sound was real. What if there was something dangerous down there, a potential threat?

For a moment, I lay back down and thought about waking up my real body. I've always been able to control dreams before they veer to an uncomfortable place. But I stopped myself. I stood back up. This feeling of being in two worlds was too bizarre not to explore. Because I had somehow created this state, I wondered if I could go further. I wondered if I could fly.

I lifted my body up. Sure enough, it elevated. *Yes, I can*, I thought. *I can fly.* I flew around the comforts of the majestic alcove. The cave was as large as a football field. The feeling was amazing, if not totally believable to me.

When I started to lie back down, I could still feel the fire. But before I lost this ability, whatever it was, wherever it was coming from, I decided I should explore.

I looked up at the sky. There was a three-quarter moon, so I knew the desert would be bright. I lifted my body again and began to fly.

I flew up over the canyon rim, across the desert, and through the countryside. I kept flying, over the San Bernardino Mountains, all the way to California. By the time I reached California, the sun was starting to rise.

Typically, there is a layer of smog over the San Bernardino Mountains. It was there but different. The smog had risen to the tops of the mountains and created black swirls in the sky. From above, it was the most polluted air I had ever seen. It looked like carbon exhaust that was magnified forty times to the point where I didn't think anyone could live or breathe. In the city below I didn't see any activity, not even any cars driving around. I decided to explore.

I descended. As I approached the foothills and closed in on the city, I spotted an apartment complex. The two-story building had a courtyard in the back. I landed on the walkway of the second floor. Through an open door, I heard a mother and child talking. They sounded fine. But the entire situation felt weird. The cars in the streets were all abandoned. As I walked toward the door, I heard somebody walking up the stairs.

I reached the door and leaned into the apartment. I saw that the mother and child were in the kitchen. They were occupied with something and turned away from me, so I decided to enter and slip by them. Despite knowing I was dreaming, I didn't want to get caught because I was unsure what the repercussions would be.

As I made my way through the apartment, I saw there was a screen open, so I went out the back to the courtyard. Once in the courtyard, I decided to depart. But the courtyard had wooden latticework around the top. I flew around like a trapped bird looking for a break in the lattice. All the while, I still felt the fire on my left shoulder.

The fire kept me focused. I knew I had to return to my real body. I found a gap in the lattice, squeezed through it, and returned to my cave faster than I had arrived. Back in my real body on terra firma, I opened up my eyes. The fire was crackling in front of me, real as could be.

I sat up, dumbfounded and bewildered by the whole experience. I didn't want to analyze it, so I lay back down and fell asleep.

I woke up the next morning, the fifth day after the fourth night, when visions typically occur. The vision was over; my awareness was heightened. I didn't know what to make of the experience, but I did know it portended well for me. It was time to return to my tasks of the journey.

I had collected a couple of squirrel skins that I wanted to sew into pouches. I decided to go out and hunt some more squirrels. I also wanted to make a bone awl. The area was pretty void of bones, but I remembered one cave where I thought I might find an old cow bone.

I walked to the cave where I thought bones might be. I entered and walked the length of the cave but didn't see a single bone. Right as I was on my way out, I saw one little white speck in the sand. I reached down, flicked the speck, and saw there was more buried there. I kept digging. Two feet underground, I felt something and spread out the sand to have a look.

I uncovered what was certainly an ancient, thousand-year-old Anasazi bone awl, perfectly made. Six inches in length, the awl was carefully made from the femur of a deer. The tool's maker had split it from a section of the femur and ground it down. It was still sharp. The craftsmanship was exceptional. The person had done a far better job than I could do.

I ended up using that bone awl for the next two weeks until a cave took it away. It disappeared into the sand again. Small things such as awls often get lost in the sand and disappear easily. The bone awl was left to be discovered again.

To this day, I still don't understand the significance of the vision I had of the mother and child in their apartment with a virtual wasteland surrounding them. There are possibilities. I don't know if it is part of my life that is yet to be lived, or something that I will discover affecting someone else's life. Perhaps it is as a simple as the fact that a night gave me something intangible that I had never seen (the flying scene), and the following morning gave me something tangible that I had never seen (the bone awl).

The awl was like finding a needle in a haystack. To this day, none of my friends has ever found an Anasazi awl. I just happened to walk out that morning needing to find a bone to make an awl. Those awls exist in museums and ancient burial grounds, but to stumble on one randomly in a cave is a one-in-a-billion chance. That led me to tie the discovery to the vision I had.

I do know that visions make it possible for me to be alone for long periods of time. They make me feel that there is a greater being watching over. They make me feel that I am not alone. As such, they have become an essential part of survival.

Visions have allowed me to discover that I can confidently live alone for extended periods of time with no human contact. But rather than feeling alone during those times, I actually feel more connected. Many survivalists who spend time in nature feel as though they have to read to keep themselves from losing all touch with others. Absorbing the stories from the pages keeps them from feeling alone. But I found that if you don't read, then you can open yourself up to visions that ultimately make you feel even more connected to life.

Chapter Sixteen

THE SOLSTICE JOURNEY

Though I had been teaching survival skills courses and leading hunter-gatherer trips for ten years, I felt that I was lacking a bigger piece to the puzzle. Despite the fact that I had spent weeks and even months at a time in the wilderness, I couldn't impart to students what truly living in the wilderness meant. I had to experience it for myself.

As an instructor who regularly took people out on monthlong hunter-gatherer trips, I was seeing in both myself and my students that we were making headway toward a place on a physical, spiritual, and mental spot, but then it would just end. I wanted to break those barriers and see what it was like to be out for an extended period of time.

At the time, I was thirty-three. I was feeling a lack of discipline in my life in terms of setting goals and sticking with them. At times, I felt like a wanderer in need of grounding. In the wilderness, one of the most critical things you must learn is how to be spontaneous and turn on a dime. Even if you make a plan, you have to be able to adjust that plan in seconds. Plans can be dangerous. You don't know when it's going to storm, when you are going to come across the next animal, or when natural obstacles will alter where you camp.

As I tried to carry that philosophy through my life, I was always adjusting and changing on a dime, sometimes to the point where, honestly, there were days when I needed to make a decision, but I couldn't. I was feeling indecisive with my life, so I sat down in the spring and wrote out a few goals on a piece of paper.

The biggest goal was to take a journey. I wrote down that I would go out for three months. Then I thought that was too short. I put it down for six months—from winter solstice to summer solstice. I had been out in the wilderness for extended periods, such as on the revised all-primitive walk. But on all those journeys, I would occasionally come across a town or some other aspects of modern civilization. The goal of the Solstice Journey would be not only to live in the wilds but also not to venture into a town at all, to never spend a dollar, and not to use any modern resources.

Questions swirled about my capabilities as a survivalist. How long could I live alone in the wilderness with no connection to society? What would I learn? How would it change me? What would it do to me physically, to my skills, to the whole collective picture of my core as a survivalist?

As I wrestled with these questions, I came to the conclusion that I needed to find answers even if it cost me my life—though my time in the wilderness had made me confident enough in my abilities that I could survive and even thrive pretty much anywhere.

Throughout the summer teaching season, I became more and more excited about the prospect of the journey. But at the same time, I was also nervous. I had been very comfortable going out in the fall and staying out for a couple weeks or a month. But the thought of going out in the middle of winter, the absolute hardest time of the year, and committing to stay out for six months with no human interaction whatsoever was daunting.

Setting the journey's starting point at the winter solstice gave me time after the teaching season ended to mentally prepare, and also to gather food and make any clothes and supplies. I was living in a cone-shaped wickiup on BOSS land that was only large enough for my body and one other person if need be. I had lived there for two years. It was a small brush hut with a fire area in front of it, but it served as a nice base to prepare for the journey.

I packed as sparingly as possible for the journey. I had a canvas back-pack that I loaded up with everything I could, but I tried not to take too many gadgets. I took one set of regular clothes, moccasins, a coyote-skin blanket, and a down blanket. I took a saw and a machete, along with feathers and fletching to make arrows and extra hides to work on. On my feet were running shoes.

For food, I loaded up basic rations of rice, lentils, olive oil, nuts, seeds, as well as dried fruit and dried greens. I also brought dried nee-dles, mint, and acorns. I packed three pounds of fresh meat and about fifteen pounds of dried elk meat. It was enough to get me started for the winter, and about all I could carry.

As I contemplated the journey, my emotions were running high. I was scared because I knew how important this goal was to my life as an instructor. If, for some reason, I didn't complete the journey, I felt that it would strip my life of validity.

I had reached a crossroads. I was at a point where I said to myself, I can't teach long-term survival skills if I don't have the ability to do it on my own—which meant the ability to complete the six-month Solstice Journey. But I was afraid. I was afraid that if I returned short of my goal, my spirit to teach would be crushed for years. If that were the case, I would be forced to justify the path of my life.

I had already gained a reputation among many in my community as the best hunter-gatherer and primitive-skills teacher in the Western

Hemisphere. For me to not be able to accomplish a goal that on the surface for someone like me seemed fairly simple would have been unacceptable. I would be devastated. I knew that if I did not make it, my life would go in a different direction. Maybe I would have to quit teaching and do something else—like go into television.

On the winter solstice, the shortest day of the year, I walked into the wilderness in Southern Utah with the goal of living there for six months. The day I left it was snowing. The land seemed to be reaching out to me. It wasn't very cold, and the snow added a beautiful white carpet, too. I hiked through mounting snowdrifts out into the backcountry.

About eight miles from town, I set up a base camp. I built a wickiup that was larger than the one I lived in. The wickiup is basically a low tepee built out of bark and debris with walls that are thick and insulated naturally. The one on BOSS land wasn't large enough to have a fire inside, but I knew that a fire would be key to surviving the subfreezing nights.

The traditional brush structure would serve as home base. It took several days to gather the materials and rough in the frame and another week to layer the bark and debris for the walls. Knowing that the temperature would drop to below zero at night, I built walls that were four feet thick. The insulation consisted of a mishmash of sticks, debris, bark, and pine needles. The end result was perfect. Every night as I lay down to sleep I would giggle because I had such a nice house.

I had previously built wickiups large enough to make a fire inside. They draft really well because they naturally breathe throughout, unlike a tepee. In a tepee, the venting comes up the side under the liner; whereas the entire wickiup is porous. When I built this wickiup, I completely closed the top to hold in the heat. At first, it appeared to draft fine, but after about three weeks, I developed a cough.

The issue was that the air was not circulating fast enough. I did two things to remedy my cough. First, I crawled up to the top and pulled debris aside to open a hole in the top. Though the structure immediately became cooler, the hole eliminated the smoke. However, on some nights, it was so cold—I later learned that temperatures dipped into the minus-ten-degree range—that I sacrificed my lungs for a night. Over time, I adjusted the size of the hole to regulate the temperature.

I also became more careful with the type of wood I burned. I started using more sagebrush and cottonwood versus oak, which was a bit harder on my lungs. In experimenting, I learned that pine wasn't great on my lungs, either, but the oak was the worst.

Every other morning, I would wake up and jump in the partially frozen creek and then come back to dry off in front of a warm fire. On other mornings, to keep me warm enough I would go on a long run and use the heat generated from my body to jump into the creek. After that daily ritual, I would meditate.

The journey had phases. The initial shock was jolting. Realizing it was going to be such a long period of time, I began experiencing feelings of loneliness. I had just enough food that I was not starving, but I was extremely hungry every day in the beginning. I spent a lot of time conserving energy by meditating on the hilltop, doing yoga, and writing and reflecting. Time began to lose its relevance.

During the first month, to stretch out my provisions I ate one meal a day. I spent my waking hours working on arts and crafts. I built several hunting tools and also worked on turning some skins that I had brought into extra clothing. Twice a week, I would fish. Every other day, I would hike ten miles to explore the land and return at night.

The only person I saw in the first month was Dave Neesha, a close friend of mine who had a camp a couple miles away. He was out for forty days. Oddly, knowing that Dave was camped a half mile away with his girlfriend made those feelings worse because I seldom saw him. It would have been easier not knowing someone was near me.

After Dave left, I didn't see anyone for two and a half months.

As I started settling into the land, the feelings of loneliness dissipated. All my senses became heightened. I was flowing with the land. I was hearing more, seeing more, feeling more, and the land was communicating with me. Once that happened, I lost the pangs of loneliness.

At night, I read benign nature textbooks. Normally on a walkabout, I wouldn't bring books, so as to keep the world out. But on this journey, I wanted to have something to keep me company. I didn't want to end up drawing a face on a rock and pouring out my heart to it. I read nature books and guides on tracking and plants. Though the books were not engaging in the least, I ended up reading each one six or seven times. To this day, I still remember nearly every word of text.

I also had a tiny AM/FM radio. I turned it on only every now and then. For some reason, the radio only worked at night and even then not very well. Over fuzzy reception, I would hear callers pouring out their hearts about being lonely. If I had a phone, I might have called in and given them a real earful on being alone.

The entire time I probably said five sentences aloud. I would say to myself things like, "I have to get up. I need to gather food. The leak in the shelter has to be mended." Every once in a while, I would hum or sing just to have the soothing feeling of my voice coming through my throat. But carrying on a dialogue with myself seemed weird. I also never had any desire to talk to a rock, a tree, or a pinecone.

It was wintertime. By then in a native culture, people would have procured and stored their meat. Winter is not an ideal time to gather meat, or anything else, for that matter. I managed to find some onions and spiderwort, which is still available that time of year. Every morning, I would make pine-needle-and-yucca tea. But for the first month, I mostly lived on the rations I had brought.

My body felt mostly normal during this time. Though I lost about ten pounds over the first two months, I still felt strong. I had no noticeable physical issues or changes.

And then wham!

Just beyond the two-month mark, there was a cataclysmic shift. I believe it was a mental trigger than took me down physically. Because I had originally set the goal at three months and then changed it to six, I kept thinking that if I had stuck to three months, I'd be on my way back to enjoy a big meal, see my friends, and listen to music. Instead, somewhat frighteningly, I was three months from returning home and my body felt like it was shutting down.

I had zero strength. My whole body felt like it was full of lead. Because I was pretty lean to begin with, I had become emaciated. If someone saw me, they would've thought I was starving to death. Maybe I was. In the mornings, it took every ounce of energy just to get up and gather food.

The following two to three weeks going into the third month were the lowest point. I was trapped in an out-and-out survival situation. I reached the point where I didn't know if I would pull through. During that time, I limited my movements. I forced myself to conserve every bit of energy I had.

I barely had the strength to file a dart or work on any type of craft. In the afternoon, I would try to hunt. Every once in a while I would spear a rabbit, though only maybe once a week in my depleted state. My energy was so low that I wasn't able to cover the distance I needed to come across animals.

My savior was that my fishing skills were still tuned to the point where I could sense where fish were and hit them with a spear blindfolded. I knew that if I pushed myself to walk down to the creek, I could toss my spear and land a few fish.

On the days that I fished, I would also collect greens for salad. I would return to camp and cook the fish. I would then wilt the salad greens, put the cooked fish on top, and add a little olive oil. That became my second meal of the day.

I was sleeping fifteen to sixteen hours a day. When I woke up in the morning, my body—despite the fact that I was probably down to 140 pounds at that point—felt like it weighed 1,400 pounds. I felt like I had lost at least thirty pounds, which sounds like a lot, but I had seen students lose that much weight in a month. On survival treks, people can lose a pound a day. My arms and legs felt like lead. I have never felt them so heavy. My eyes would open in the morning, but I couldn't even lift my head off the ground. I would roll over, muster every ounce of strength, and push my body up. Once I was in a sitting position, my head would begin to spin.

After an hour, I would finally stand. I would walk down to the creek and collect the food I needed, as virtually all my initial rations were gone. Bending over was draining, but somehow I managed to pick greens. I would steam a large portion—more than most people could eat in one sitting—in a clay pot. Then I would make pine needle tea. At the end of the meal I was so tired, I had to lie down and rest.

For several days, even weeks, I didn't know what was going on with my body. I felt certain that my body was shutting down and I was slowly dying. If I did die, I reasoned that I would not die a fraud. I was either going to complete these six months alone and return to my life as a teacher of primitive-living skills, or die. There was no third option.

After three weeks in that heavily depleted state, I slowly started to feel stronger. As fit as I was entering the wilderness, I now realize that there were leftover toxins that I needed to expunge. Though I ate healthy when I was in society, my diet contained carbs and other sources of energy that hunter-gatherers don't consume on a regular basis.

My metabolism had also slowed down because I was eating less. This made it far more efficient and meant that I didn't have to eat as often. Americans eat constantly, so if we don't eat every four hours, our blood sugar drops and we feel woozy. When you reach the point where I was, even if you don't eat for a couple days, your blood sugar remains stable.

Coming out of the energy crash, I felt like I was in a living situation rather than a survival situation. I began to notice intriguing, positive physical changes.

I could smell things I'd never smelled before and hear things I'd never heard before. Walking through the canyon, I could pick up the scent of an old track or an animal that was out of sight. When I was fishing, I could hear fish cutting through the water. Even though I couldn't see the fish, I could actually tell how big it was and which direction it was heading from the sound.

I felt as if I had finally achieved a hunter-gatherer body. I had very little body fat, and concentrated muscle tissue. I could go for a couple days without eating much at all. I felt super-light, and I could move like a wild animal.

But perhaps the most inexplicable change was that the tartar literally started peeling off my teeth in chunks. Initially, it left a sour taste in my mouth. However, I noticed that when all the tartar had flaked off, I had a sweet, calming taste in my mouth.

I also had a small black hole that looked like a cavity in one of my rear teeth. For months, it had caused occasional pain. But the pain subsided as the tartar flaked off. One day, I looked at the tooth in my compass mirror. There was a stain on the enamel where the hole had been, but the hole was gone. It somehow seemed to have repaired itself. I have no idea how, and the spot never returned.

Later, I told a dentist what had happened. The dentist poked at it and said there was a spot under the enamel but no cavity. I was told that it takes seven years of a dedicated diet of high greens and meat and zero sugar for enamel to repair itself. The natural world had done that in two months.

In April, the fourth month of my Solstice Journey, I crossed over the final threshold of survival. The three-month point—the original goal—had come and gone. My strength had returned, and I knew my six-month goal was feasible. Mentally, physically, and emotionally, I was all in.

I have found that when I first put myself in a new situation, the loneliness is adjusted to the time frame. For example, if someone were to go out for four days in a similar situation, they would probably feel very lonely the first day. On the second day, they would begin to get into a groove. Then on the third day, they would feel great because the journey was nearly over. But because I was going to be out six months, I put that issue on the back burner.

I had never been in a survival situation for that length of time. I also was well aware of the challenge. When I started, I had only a month and a half's supply of food. That meant for several months I would have to live solely off the land. Prior to the Solstice Journey, the longest I had lived exclusively off the land was about forty days.

Admittedly, I was nervous about it, not because I didn't think I could succeed, but because I didn't want to have to return to town and answer questions about why I was back so soon. I had told everyone I knew that I was going out for six months, both to let them know where I was so they wouldn't worry and to mentally align myself to the challenge.

The final three months were almost otherworldly on many levels. Spring had arrived. The weather became noticeably warmer and the earth was coming alive. Part of the feeling emanated from the fact that I had made it through winter. The animals were coming out of their hiding places and returning to their daily routines. The plants were starting to push through the soil. Mustard greens were opening up, and the watercress was thickening.

I started to wander the land, traveling light. I would leave my base for weeks at a time. Some days I would cover thirty to forty miles. Using both the sun and the land features, such as the unique rock formations or large bunches of nettles, I would find my way back.

I could also roam with ease. I didn't have to stay in my shelter. My strength started to return, a welcome feeling after the scare I initially encountered. I felt an enjoyment I hadn't felt in some time. I began to make daily circles through the canyons, and ultimately covered hundreds of miles. I spent time in the Kaiparowits hunting and foraging for food. I'd gather greens, hunt rabbits, and trap squirrels.

The first time I left my home base, I was away for two weeks. I returned for a few days, and then was gone again for six or so weeks.

I roamed the Kaiparowits, which is about 110 square miles. Though roads intersect it, there are ways to parallel the roads for long distances if you know the terrain. The sad truth is that anywhere you are in the United States, you will be within thirty miles of a dirt or paved road. However, if you know the land as well as I know Southern Utah, you can parallel the road. Because of that, I crossed a highway only twice the entire six months.

The stress of keeping time was completely removed. I didn't measure time in any conventional way. It was almost easier to lose track of time and settle into the experience. Counting the days by nicking a log sounds like survival. It's akin to the guy who gets lost counting the days until he is rescued. For me, that would have driven me nuts.

I was able to keep track of a month passing by the moon, as I knew that from one full moon to the next was a month, but I was a week or two off in either direction until spring grew near and told me the time of year. Even in the spring, I would wake up and think, *It's probably late March, possibly even April.* When I ran into a hiker toward the end of the six months—only the second human I had seen in four months—I asked him what day it was. When he told me it was June 6, I started keeping track of the days because I was so close to the end.

By the end of June, I was mostly ready to return. From a practical standpoint, I was scheduled to teach that summer and needed to prepare. I was ready to see friends and return to my life. Yet I was also wondering what would happen to me on a physical, mental, and emotional level if I stayed out for a year.

For one, it would be easier. June 21 to December 21 is the posh time of the year to live off the land. Summer reaps the rewards of spring's work, and the fall is especially productive because that time of year wants to give you a lot before winter comes.

But it was time to return. I had achieved my goal. I felt like I could continue with my life's pursuits honestly.

On June 20, two days before the summer solstice, I walked toward Boulder. I had my supplies in a buckskin bag I had made from skins I brought with me and tanned. When I reached the top of a sandstone peak, I could see Boulder. It was but an hour's walk. But I stopped because it wasn't the twenty-first, and cheating my goal at this point seemed rather ridiculous.

That night I looked out at the lights of the houses and farms dotting the landscape. Civilization was below me, but in no way did I feel above it. I felt humbled. I lay down under my blanket and fell into a gentle sleep.

I awoke just as the sun was coming up and the lights were going off. I packed up and walked to the BOSS grounds, where my wickiup home was. I had a couple handfuls of nonbiodegradable trash in a small bag. It contained a couple cans, some plastic, and dead batteries from the reading lamp I had taken. My six-month footprint on the earth was not even a pinkie print.

When I discarded the trash, I remember thinking I had created more trash than that in a day, and many people create more in an hour. That was very rewarding. For six months, I had lived with the land and improved the land. I harvested from plants in a way that improved their growth. I hunted animals in a way that preserved plants for other animals and sustained the cycle of life. I had emerged with only a small bag of trash.

When I reached the BOSS grounds, I walked into the office. Several staff members were mulling around, typing on their laptops. It was a weird sight. When I had left six months earlier, most people at the school were decidedly antitechnology. Though I had been gone only six months, I was able to immediately see what I considered a radical change that others would later describe as an unnoticeable transition.

Steve Dessinger, a staff member and friend of mine, was sitting at the desk closest to the door. He looked up from his computer and said, "Oh, hi, Matt." And then he looked back down and continued working.

I paused for a moment, swept my eyes around the room. No one else even noticed me. I stepped back outside and went to my wickiup to unpack. As I unloaded, I couldn't help but think that was a rather perfunctory hello to give someone after they had been gone for six months in the wild.

Later that night, everyone threw a party for me. There were hugs all around. Even Steve acted like he was seeing me for the first time. Each person approached me differently about the journey. Some people noted that I looked very skinny, like I had barely survived. There were plenty of jokes as well, particularly about my mental state. One guy said, "Wow, you don't even seem crazy." My friend Mojo pushed me for spiritual answers, which I could not properly convey.

I ate plentifully and healthfully. The only thing I had missed was ice cream. After being back for a couple days, I had some ice cream—which I dearly regretted. It made me not feel so good. Ice cream had always been my one weakness, my one craving when I was on the trail. So my Solstice Journey had another unintended consequence: it got me over ice cream.

Aside from that, along with the incredible physical and mental journey, there were spiritual aspects to living alone for so long, and they have informed the person that I am and become part of my teachings. Few people, if any, spend that much time alone. I had no idea what I would do if I had a heart attack. During that time, I actually felt clearer, and in odd ways even more articulate despite the fact that there was no one to talk to. When I came out, I was much clearer and more concise with everyone I spoke to.

There were benefits small and large to living in the wild as I did. I never got sick. It's impossible to catch a cold or a fever in the wild because there are no people to transmit them. Injuries were also not a concern. Most people get injured when they sit around at a desk, or in a car or airplane, and then explode out of them into a flurry of activity. But in the wilderness, even on the least productive days, I am constantly moving to the point where my body is always prepared for the next task. The muscles stay looser and more nimble.

Once in a while I would do yoga, but I never stretched. I didn't need to. People always say they feel old after they exert themselves. But the fact is that they merely *feel* old because they sit around, then they are active, and then they sit around again. There is a reason why Australian aboriginal hunter-gatherers, old men who are eighty, are chucking a spear the day before they die. They are physically active and remain uninjured their whole lives because they maintain a steadiness and an evenness to the physical tasks in their lives.

Those six months were the happiest time of my life—despite the fact that I almost died after the first three months. I felt so tuned in to and in touch with everything. Not having a backpack of modern supplies makes you inherently more dependent on nature. This is something we can apply to our lives. When we find ourselves in an unfamiliar situation or in a new city, we tend to go with what is most familiar, rather than reaching out and touching that new situation in a physical or even psychological way.

I found that I tapped into parts of me that I didn't know were there, and lessons that could be applied to my life sprang from them. For example, one day I would notice the colors of the leaves on the cottonwood trees. The next day I noticed the colors were duller, even though the sun and clouds were the same. This puzzled me. What had happened to my perceptions? The next day, the color returned.

What that told me was that nobody perceives things the same way. The way you see red may be different from the way I see red. This helped me to reserve judgments against people, because I came to understand that they might have different perceptions than me.

Looking back, the Solstice Journey was the single most important event in my life. For those six months I had a goal that was simple and to the point: to not come into a town or civilization. I knew that returning even for a day would be a huge distraction.

People are always interested in what I packed and if I had any human contact. Some are looking for inspiration through my journey. Others want to poke holes in my experience. But that does not bother me. The journey was about maintaining as much of a nature connection as humanly possible.

That time showed me, in some way, how nature thinks. I got into her mind in a way that I think very few humans can.

EPIC SURVIVAL RULE #5:

LEARN FROM OTHERS

I am no longer afraid to fail, because failure no longer means death. If I fail, I can learn from it and use that in my teaching. I am chasing survival and catching it.

The things I am learning from devoting my life to the wilderness cannot be picked up from reading a book. The only way to learn them is to live fully in the wilderness. As I do that, I feel like I will be better able to show this real world to others who live in the man-made, artificial world, and that will make their lives fuller.

After experiencing the wilderness through climbing and running, I have over time learned the necessary skills to live in the wild: tracking animals, crafting stone and bone tools, building shelters, and making fire with friction. I am now applying those skills to the most extreme survival situations and turning them into living situations.

I hope I'm far enough along that I can translate what I know to others who don't live in the wilderness. In everyday life, it is easy to get caught up in yourself. The land does not allow that. It demands that you look around and observe. Now that I am able to completely observe the physical aspects of the land itself, I am doing that in my own relationships. When I am with people, I find myself thinking, Okay, what does my friend need today? What do I need to do to be better for this person?

The lessons of the wilderness are feeling more and more applicable to everyday life outside the wilderness. Like other people who become proficient in their fields and help others, I feel like I am entering a new phase of my life from which others can benefit.

Chapter Seventeen

SURVIVAL TOOLS

H unting tools are essential to the survivalist. They are necessary to gather food to keep you nourished while living in the wilderness. But they also become a part of you and one of the defining aspects of your respect for the land.

The first thing to understand about any survival tool—whether it is a hunting tool, blanket, piece of clothing, or fire to keep you warm—is that you must establish a connection to the earth to have a pure experience with it.

At first, it may seem foolish to trade out your lighter for a friction fire kit or your sleeping bag for a wool blanket, or take your knife out of its sheath and make a leather one—or better yet, leave your knife behind and learn how to use tools made from stone. Maybe you can even create your own clothing.

In the beginning, you may suffer, but you will never experience the layers of survival if you don't try. The layers have always existed. A hunter-gatherer leaving the village to go on a vision quest could be the equivalent of a backpacker leaving all the last gadgets behind to establish a deeper connection in the woods. This is not to say that people should not go out on the land with their backpacks full of gear, if that is what they love to do. Natural tools may be harder, but they also may be more fulfilling.

There is a complex simplicity involved in the making of all hunting tools. Every region of the globe has had many generations of tool crafts-men to evolve the hunting tools that work best in that landscape. The list of primitive tools is extensive. They include the spear, the blowgun, the bolo, the sling, the throwing club, the rabbit stick, the bow, the boomer-ang, and most historically, the atlatl.

The atlatl and the bow are similar. Both project a "missile" toward the target. The atlatl is generally smaller and the rope attached to the dart makes it ideal for fishing, while the bow (and arrow) is better suited for shooting game over distance. The boomerang is most effective on open terrain.

The most versatile of all hunting tools is the atlatl. An atlatl is a de-vice for throwing a spear that gives it greater velocity. The atlatl creates an extra joint to the arm. It throws like a cross between a javelin and an elongated arrow.

Much of the information I have learned about tools and hunting has come from trial and error—an atlatl that backfires can maim you if you're not careful—and from studying what others have done. All teach-ers should be students, because there are no absolutes.

Having the right balance of tools allows you to draw energy from the land and gather food in extreme circumstances. Developing a sense of the land is crucial to being able to build and ultimately use the tools properly. These hunting tools require a clear sense of mind and an awareness of animals to be effective, and they must become an extension of the hunter. Experiencing that connection is powerful. It can also determine whether you live or die in the wilderness.

The first thing to understand about primitive hunting tools is that you can't just step into a survival situation and make a primitive bow, atlatl, or boomerang or any other tool and expect to hunt effectively with them if you have never used them before.

It takes a week to dial in to that tool. You can't speed up the process and be successful. The atlatl is the only tool I have been able to make and use on the fly to catch small game. But making a bow is a process. I've never known anybody who has made a bow and caught something in the same week. The bow doesn't have that quality.

To make an effective bow, you must cure the bow. You can speed up that process by doing it over a fire for a couple days, but it still must be cured. To make the arrows, you essentially have to follow the same process. However, if they are rapid cured, the spines will not be what you are used to. So even in a survival situation, someone who has a great deal of skill and experience will need four days minimum to get something dialed in—to say nothing of learning about the land where you need to use it.

While the boomerang works far better when it is cured, it is possible to make one that is "green" and use it. The boomerang is inherently easier because it can be used to go after a flock of animals, thereby lessening the skill needed to make a kill.

For the average person in a survival situation who has never used any hunting tools, the boomerang, club, and spear are the best options. Those would be followed by traps. In a pure survival situation, the simplest tools are the more effective for the average person.

The fact is that it takes years of dedication to know how to create and use a tool properly. The defining quality to hunting tools created from the land is that they are very specific to that landscape. For instance, a long bow works well in one environment while it doesn't work great in another. Same with a short bow. Hunting boomerangs are the same, depending on the type of game you are hunting.

As the archaeological records of mankind show, the atlatl has been used longer than any other hunting tool. It is responsible for us being alive. Ancient European cultures used it for ten thousand years before they decided to start using a bow.

The atlatl has gained a reputation for its ability to kill woolly mammoths. But the fact is that the atlatl was not used just to kill woolly mammoths and then put away once the mammoths were extinct. It was used as the primary and sole hunting tool up to a thousand years ago when this continent had the exact same game as it does now.

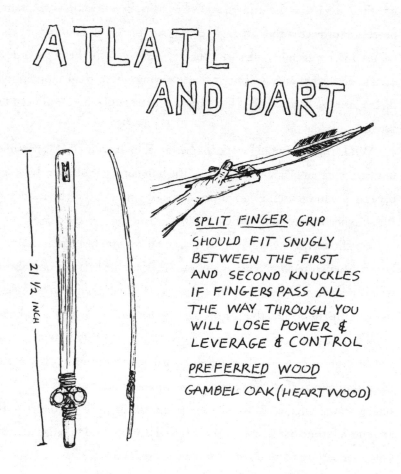

ATLATL AND DART

21 ½ INCH

SPLIT FINGER GRIP
SHOULD FIT SNUGLY
BETWEEN THE FIRST
AND SECOND KNUCKLES
IF FINGERS PASS ALL
THE WAY THROUGH YOU
WILL LOSE POWER &
LEVERAGE & CONTROL

PREFERRED WOOD
GAMBEL OAK (HEARTWOOD)

Many people think that once the bow came into existence, it was the superior tool and people simply stopped using the atlatl. That's far from the case. Once the bow was employed, there continued to be an overlap. Even in our records of when the bow was first starting to be used and understood, that same tribe often preferred the atlatl. The bow for a long time was considered a tinker toy or a very specialized shooting weapon.

Though the bow and atlatl appear to be similar, there are differences. The advantage to a bow is that there is very little movement involved in its use. The lack of movement from the hunter to flag an animal when he takes a shot allows him to slowly draw back the bow. When he releases the arrow, he is not waving his hand toward the target, as he would be while throwing an atlatl. Actually, in my opinion that's the only modern advantage to a bow over an atlatl. In primitive times, using a bow also allowed people to carry a quiver of arrows for going to war, as they obviously could not retrieve a dart in battle.

A D bow is about sixty inches long. In Southern Utah, the best materials for making the bow are Gambel oak, Russian olive, and serviceberry. However, I prefer other materials, such as juniper and ash. Those make a better bow with sinew. I have since learned that maple also makes an effective D bow.

The bow's string is a two-ply twist sinew that is loosened with saliva, finger rolled on a log, and then stretched between two trees. The tip of the arrow varies. A long tip is used for a quick kill, whereas a stone tip is used for a stun.

Though bows are very much in favor, I prefer the atlatl to the bow because it is very Zen. People talk about archery as being Zen, but once you throw an atlatl accurately there is nothing that will create that kind of focus and meditation. Using a bow and arrow has a Zen feeling because you are controlling your muscles to stabilize the shot. Once you reach that point, you aim and let go. But with the atlatl, you put your entire body into it. That teaches harmony and helps you reach it.

BOW AND ARROWS

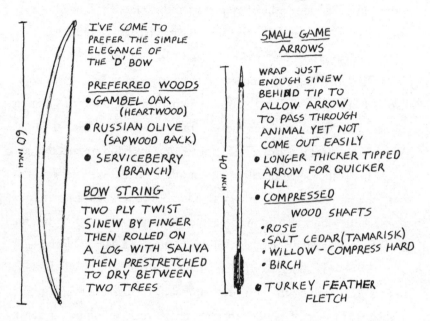

I'VE COME TO PREFER THE SIMPLE ELEGANCE OF THE 'D' BOW

PREFERRED WOODS
● GAMBEL OAK
      (HEARTWOOD)
● RUSSIAN OLIVE
      (SAPWOOD BACK)
● SERVICEBERRY
      (BRANCH)

BOW STRING
TWO PLY TWIST SINEW BY FINGER THEN ROLLED ON A LOG WITH SALIVA THEN PRESTRETCHED TO DRY BETWEEN TWO TREES

SMALL GAME ARROWS

WRAP JUST ENOUGH SINEW BEHIND TIP TO ALLOW ARROW TO PASS THROUGH ANIMAL YET NOT COME OUT EASILY
● LONGER THICKER TIPPED ARROW FOR QUICKER KILL
● COMPRESSED
      WOOD SHAFTS
● ROSE
● SALT CEDAR (TAMARISK)
● WILLOW - COMPRESS HARD
● BIRCH
● TURKEY FEATHER
      FLETCH

60 INCH

40 INCH

Archaeological records and studies show that nothing uses more explosive brainpower than throwing an object, even in our frenetic technologically driven society. For that split second, throwing an object requires the greatest amount of concentration a human can muster, without exception.

The atlatl becomes an extension of your arm, the tool an extra joint in your body. The dart itself becomes spiritually and physically connected to you in some way. As you practice throwing it, you start to "know" the dart. Throwing a rock would be very Zen if you kept the same rock all the time. But people don't do that. They go down to a creek and start chucking rocks. The first rock is no different from the sixth. However, if you retrieved the first rock every time you threw it, you would become attached to that rock, and it would become an extension of your hand and your arm.

The dart becomes a part of you because after you throw it, you collect it. Eventually, you start developing a relationship with that particular dart. You understand the way it flies, how it reacts to natural obstacles, such as wind and rain. If you stick with that same dart long enough, you will know it so well that you will be hitting dimes out of the air—or at least a pinecone from ten yards.

Darts are also more durable, so they last longer than arrows, which is helpful while practicing and hunting. The dart can be crafted from any type of stiff, thin piece of wood that has enough flex to give it the proper flight. Cane is a great source for that, as are willows and birch.

Depending on the continent, the atlatl itself has many different shapes and designs. The Eskimos used a one-finger design that had a very neutral hand position. They primarily used it for hunting on the ocean shores, meaning that they just needed a straight down flick to hit a fish or a seal. Unlike the bow, which is inevitably bent to a slight imperfection, the atlatl can be made to be ergonomically perfect.

I made my first atlatl shortly after I moved to Boulder. It was based on a drawing I saw in Larry Dean Olsen's book *Outdoor Survival Skills*. I worked very hard to perfect the design and spent hours practicing with it, but I could never get that atlatl to fly correctly. Based on my limited trial and error and the impatience of youth, I dismissed the tool altogether. For years, I considered the atlatl to be outdated, impractical, and even silly.

Several years passed before I tried again. I read more books about the use of the atlatl in primitive times, and I studied different models that had evolved over centuries. I came to the conclusion that I had made a crappy model. It wasn't worthy of flight, and certainly not of leading a hunt. I decided to try again.

Using a picture of an atlatl from the Southern Utah area, where I felt most connected to the land, I constructed a different atlatl. I reasoned that what worked thousands of years ago in my area should work now. Again, I was met with frustration. Though this atlatl worked better, I was not satisfied with its flight, nor did I feel any connection to the tool.

I decided to do some homework. I gathered every book and photo of all models of atlatl from aboriginal times—models from my area to the Great Lakes region to Arizona. I built several replicas of each one. In all, I ended up making about thirty atlatls. All of them were beautifully finished and delicately constructed. I then began throwing those atlatls until I decided which one fit me the best. The winner ended up being a slight hybrid to one that had been used in my area a century earlier, built in what is called the Basketmaker style.

The Basketmaker atlatl uses a six-to-eight-foot dart with a four-pronged tip. The dart has what appears to be a traditional arrow fletching on it, though in fact it is more streamlined. The grip on the Basketmaker is designed for either a baseball grip or a split-finger grip. I feel like I have more control with the split-finger grip, which fits like rings between the first and second knuckles. With the proper split-finger grip on a twenty-one-inch atlatl, I can throw a seven-foot dart farther than a hundred and fifty yards.

The models most commonly used in this area have the exact same type of arm that I use, but they have stiff loops made of sinew lines that make them rigid. The lines are covered in buckskin. Since experimenting with those, I have found a few ancient models that have handles carved from a sheep's horn. I have also used the sheep's horn specimen as a model for one I made out of hardwood.

The atlatl tip has an advantage over an arrow tip because you can place a fair bit of weight on it without making it top heavy. Hunters have used all kinds of material from splayed-out tips for fishing to barbed tips for bigger fish and small game to stone tips for big game. There were even a couple archaeological specimens with fist-size bludgeoning balls for stunning larger animals or knocking out smaller animals.

The challenge in hunting with the atlatl is how to conceal your body movement, or how to project where the animal will be by the time the dart reaches it. As an atlatl hunter who wants to put meat on the table, you are always positioning the shot in such a way that you are simultaneously evaluating the present and several seconds in the future.

Here's an example. If a rabbit ran out in front of me and stopped out in the middle of an open area, I would not take a shot at it because the rabbit would jump the shot. I would pause and follow one of two options. I would first try to figure out a way to position myself so the shot is concealed. If that were not possible, I would slowly push the rabbit into the brush so it felt more protected. Then I would take the shot into the brush.

Every hunt demands a different throw. If you were hunting game that required extra power or distance, you would develop a throw that had more length. If you were only fishing with the atlatl where you needed more control at short range, you would make a shorter throw.

There are other differences, notably in how the darts are retrieved. When fishing with a bow and arrow, I need to tie a string to the arrow or dive into the water to retrieve it after each shot. With the atlatl, I can fish in the winter without getting my feet wet. I can throw the dart from the bank, hit the fish, grab the dart, and if I have a barb on there, pull the dart back out.

FISHING DART FOR
SMALL TO MEDIUM
SIZE FISH

CANE SECTION FORESHAFT
WITH FOUR COMPRESSED
FIREHARDENED HARDWOOD
SPIKES WEDGED IN &
SPLAYED OUT

I'VE CAUGHT FISH UP
TO 15 INCH. WITH THIS
BUT CARE NEEDS TO
BE TAKEN WITH
RETRIEVAL OF
LARGER FISH – BETTER
TO USE HARPOON TIP

PREFERRED WOODS
- SERVICEBERRY
- RUSSIAN OLIVE
- WILLOW
- BIRCH
- CANE

6-8 FEET

Another reason the atlatl is better is because in deep water sometimes I will hit fish that are eight feet down. That is possible because the dart is so long that it travels fairly straight. But when an arrow shoots off a bow, it inevitably has the archer's paradox, which is flex. To a degree, both the atlatl and the arrow experience the same thing.

The archer's paradox says that the arrow is streamlined in flight, so in order to travel well, it actually has to flex around the handle of the bow and then straighten out. When an arrow hits the water, it is still bending. Depending on the direction the arrow bends, it will kick in that same direction in the water. But a dart off the atlatl, even though it somewhat does the same thing, is so long that it stabilizes and keeps driving straight through the water.

With both the arrow and the dart, there is also refraction that takes a skilled fisherman a while to learn. When the arrow (or the dart, to a lesser degree) is in the water, it's also going to appear to bend, so you need to aim below your target. When light passes from the water to the air, it bends, and that causes the fish to look like it is in a slightly different place than it actually is.

There are other distinctions between the bow and the atlatl. With the bow, even when hunting small game, you rarely make the kill shot with one arrow. This means you need at least two arrows to be an ethical hunter and likely three or four unless you have uncanny precision. With the first arrow you are hoping to hit the game in the head, but if you can't because of timing or distance, you try to hit it in the gut or the leg to disable it. Nevertheless, the animal is going to keep running. You have to grab that other arrow and make another shot. You want a dead animal; you don't want a wounded animal that gets away. With one arrow, that could easily happen; whereas, if you use an atlatl and put a dart in a small animal, the animal is not going anywhere.

There is also a distance difference between an arrow and a dart.

When using a bow, the lighter the arrow, the farther it flies. With an atlatl, what makes the dart fly farther is the thrower. Modern carbon arrows are especially lightweight, as are aluminum ones. But a proper atlatl thrower can rocket a dart past an average user of the bow who flings a lightweight arrow.

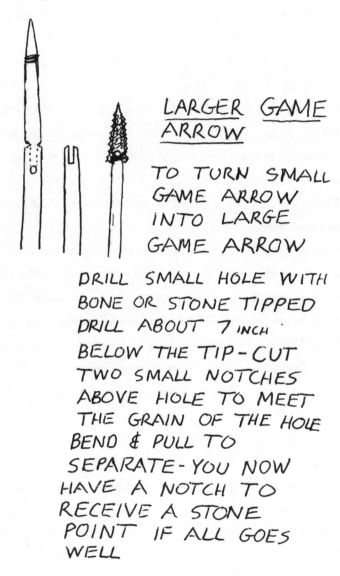

LARGER GAME ARROW

TO TURN SMALL GAME ARROW INTO LARGE GAME ARROW

DRILL SMALL HOLE WITH BONE OR STONE TIPPED DRILL ABOUT 7 INCH BELOW THE TIP-CUT TWO SMALL NOTCHES ABOVE HOLE TO MEET THE GRAIN OF THE HOLE BEND & PULL TO SEPARATE-YOU NOW HAVE A NOTCH TO RECEIVE A STONE POINT IF ALL GOES WELL

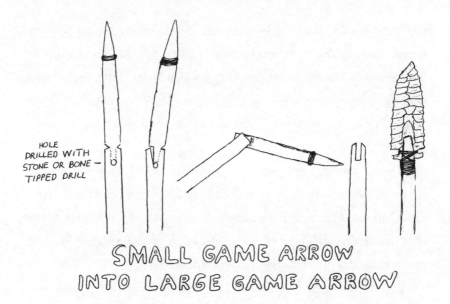

HOLE
DRILLED WITH
STONE OR BONE —
TIPPED DRILL

SMALL GAME ARROW
INTO LARGE GAME ARROW

Years ago, I was chucking darts way out across the BOSS land. Steve Dessinger, who was a program director at BOSS and eventually became its owner, was excited about how far I could throw. He asked me to try one of his lightweight aluminum darts. So I pulled back and let it go. The dart sailed way farther than either one of us anticipated. We stood there and watched as it just kept going and going. It must have traveled well over two hundred yards before it dropped into a clump of trees. We searched for an hour, but we never did find it. (Sorry, Steve.)

Watching a boomerang soar through the air and return to its thrower brings out the kid on the beach in all of us. But a hunting boomerang is far more than a toy. It is the heaviest of the three primitive tools and can inflict the most harm per throw.

A hunting boomerang is basically what it sounds like: an oversize version of a returning boomerang. The difference is that a hunting boomerang doesn't return because it is too thick and heavy. Today, specialized boomerangs are generally molded from inexpensive fibers and polycarbonate, which makes them virtually indestructible. On average, they are about twenty-eight inches long and weigh just over two pounds.

The boomerang originated with aboriginal tribes in Australia. It is best used in open terrain with very little brush or trees like the Australian Outback. However, if you throw it overhand, the boomerang can slice through tall, thick grass and brush and be very effective. A sidearm throw through grass will choke it off immediately.

The highest-quality man-made hunting boomerang is a heat-bent boomerang. An explorer named Paul Campbell taught me about these. Campbell learned the perfect construction by observing the indigenous people of California.

The construction of this boomerang is very deliberate. I take a fresh-cut sapling and heat it gently over a fire for a half hour. This allows the wood to be bent into a boomerang shape. I bend it by placing it between two trees and creating a vise. I allow the resulting boomerang to dry for two weeks before using it.

Boomerangs are best for hunting birds, particularly large ground birds. The bigger the flocks, the better. Ideally, you can catch flocks out in the open and then let the boomerang go. You hope to catch them on the ground, but even if they cluster and fly away, you can throw at that cluster. The boomerang has such a wide circumference that you will likely clip one or two of them. That was how the aborigines used boomerangs. The Hopi and Anasazi Indians in Arizona hunted quail in a similar fashion. I've also seen hunters make a clean harvest of a wild turkey with a single shot to the neck.

HUNTING BOOMERANG

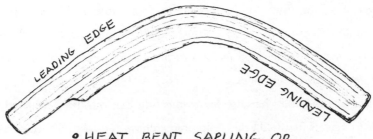

LEADING EDGE

LEADING EDGE

- HEAT BENT SAPLING OR STRAIGHT GRAINED BRANCH LET DRY THEN SHAPE
- BLUNT EDGES FOR DURABILITY NO KNOTS
- UNCUT LEADING EDGES ALSO FOR DURABILITY

PREFERRED WOODS

- OAK
- CATCLAW
- MESQUITE

Boomerangs were also used when the rabbit population swelled in Australia—hence the nickname "rabbit stick." The men would start chasing rabbits until they got a close shot and then whip the boomerang into the pack. It is also possible to chase down a single rabbit until it tires and take it with one shot.

Because of the complexity and mastery required for each tool, I stopped using the boomerang. I was feeling too spread out among the three and needed to maintain my focus on the atlatl. The closeness to the hunting tool is paramount to its success as a protein gatherer.

Whatever hunting tool a survivalist chooses must be durable enough to deliver on a hunt. But more important, it must connect with your spirit and be an extension of you. You must enjoy constructing the tool and practicing with it to develop the necessary accuracy to make you not just a hunter but also a harvester.

For me, the atlatl has also led to meeting like-minded people who want to master its use. While doing research on the atlatl, I discovered that an organization called the World Atlatl Association hosts competitions across the United States and in Europe. There are people so serious about this skill that they drive around the United States from one competition to the next trying to increase their scores. This is a pure labor of love, as there is no prize money. When I became proficient at the atlatl, I decided to test my skills in competition.

Every competition runs by the same rules. A participant throws five darts from a distance of fifteen meters, followed by another five darts from twenty meters, at a standard archery-style bull's-eye. Scoring is straightforward. The rings are worth one to ten points, a bull's-eye being ten. If you miss the target's rings, you get no points. The highest point total wins.

I have competed against and beaten the world champion on several occasions. We will usually throw five bull's-eyes at fifteen meters. At twenty meters, things are more challenging, especially if there is wind. From there, hitting a few nines is not uncommon. The trouble comes when a dart drops on you and gives you a six.

My highest score in competition was a ninety-three out of a hundred, which put me fifth in the world overall. I had actually scored a ninety-six in practice. The highest-ever score in competition is a ninety-eight. All four people ahead of me compete regularly, giving them a chance to raise their scores. But for me, the competitions were not about recognition but rather about a chance to bring me closer to my primary hunting tool.

Chapter Eighteen

HUNTING FOR A CONNECTION TO OUR FOOD

Hunting is a very sacred act that cannot be undertaken lightly. The ego must always stay in check, because the hunter is taking a life. Hunting tools should feel like an extension of the hunter and connect with his spirit. A person must also know the territory to be an effective and respectful hunter. He owes it to the land and to those creatures that have inhabited it longer than him.

To most people in our society, the act of hunting conjures up images of a guy wearing camouflage and using a rifle to shoot a wild animal. Very few modern-day hunters use primitive hunting tools. I am not opposed to people who hunt with guns. Unfortunately, when you hunt only with a gun, you have not earned it. If someone has never hunted with a primitive tool or never gone out and spent a lot of time with the animal he is hunting, then he has not developed the proper respect for the animal or for his power to take that animal's life. If a hunter picks up a rifle and pops a deer, that person has skipped a bunch of steps.

I haven't necessarily taken the easy road, but I have taken what I believe is an ethical road. I have never just picked up a hunting tool, be it a stone ax or an atlatl, and killed an animal. I have learned to make that tool, made multiple versions, and worked to understand how to use them. I have then lived in the animal's environment.

I have killed only two animals with a firearm. Friends of mine who owned expansive alfalfa fields were given five depredation tags. The authorities hand out depredation tags to people who have fields in an effort to control animal population. They asked me to help.

I, too, lived on land that contained alfalfa fields. I was given a gun during that late fall. I practiced with the gun for a week and could hit a baseball-size target at forty yards without fail.

On the day of the hunt, I stalked within twenty yards of a deer. I lined up a head shot, which would allow me a clean hide when I skinned it. That day, I shot two deer under the depredation tag guidelines.

My girlfriend Kirsten was living with me for the winter. The real upside to killing the two deer was that I would be able to preserve and store the meat for the winter for us. Had I not killed the deer, we would have gone through a long period of eating rice and beans. Together, the two of us had only three hundred dollars to make it through the winter until we started teaching again.

That was the first time I truly understood that when you are looking after a loved one, you excuse yourself for cheating the natural process to provide for them. There are many people who need to supply food, and for them the gun offers a quick and sometimes the only answer.

I don't feel that I am better than the person who goes deer hunting with a gun once or twice a year. But I believe that understanding the process of what I have created opens up my mind to different ways and techniques. Today, when I pick up a knife, it's not the same as most people picking up a knife. I appreciate the tool thoroughly—probably more so than somebody picking it up for the first or second time—but it has taken me time to go through the process.

When I hunt with an atlatl, bow, or boomerang, I feel more responsible than the time I hunted with a gun. That is purely a personal feeling, and in no way do I want to sound sanctimonious. However, hunting with my hands continues to unearth conflicted feelings.

It is hard to describe the feeling of killing something with your hands. The killing process feels horrible, yet is has a positive side. I have just killed something so I therefore feel bad about ending the life of a living thing. But I know that I will feel good in a moment when I get the nutrition I need. So I am thankful for the blessing of food from the land, but at the same time, I cannot help but show a certain amount of sorrow that I had to kill for it. That conflict will never abate.

Hunting animals respectfully is an experience in self-reliance and connections. Once in Hawaii this meant building an atlatl and hunting for a wild goat. I had observed and taken in the land for ten days. I watched the goats make their way through a streambed in the canyon. While studying the goats, I noticed that they could effortlessly navigate the hillside that was almost ninety-degree angles, but in the cobblestones of the creek bed, they had trouble finding their footing. I decided the easiest method was to run down a goat.

Grasping the atlatl in one hand, I charged the goat over the cobblestones. I chased it for a half mile, at a full sprint. I could see it was struggling. It kept slipping and sliding off the rocks. Eventually, I caught up to the goat, straddled it, grabbed its horns and pulled them back, and slit its throat.

It was traumatic. It's always emotionally tough to hold an animal in your arms and kill it. Hunters are removed when they trap an animal or shoot it—shoppers in supermarkets far more so. Despite how much I needed that meat, I literally cried my eyes out. I thanked that animal for leaving its body behind and prayed that its spirit would live on. It never gets any easier to kill something that is like me. I always accept an animal's meat as a great gift.

Every time I kill an animal—be it with a weapon, with a trap, or by hand—I say a prayer.

It's usually along the lines of "wherever your spirit may go, I hope it is a great place." But when hunting with students, I never push or enforce any spiritual concepts with them. Each person must find their own spiritual balance.

Trapping is important to surviving in the wilderness. It takes far less energy and effort than hunting, so if you are depleted, it is an easy way to get meat. In survival situations, I have trapped many different types of animals with many different traps.

I primarily teach students how to trap squirrels, because they are easy to lure. If a student has trouble, I step them down one more notch and teach them to trap mice. The easiest way to trap squirrels is to make what is called a Paiute-style deadfall. The trap is basically two slabs of rock. One of them is lifted upward with two upright sticks. Another stick is used to set a trigger mechanism that is usually baited. If you have no bait, the trap can be set over a hole. When the squirrel trips the trigger, the rock falls on its head and kills it instantly.

If students want to learn how to trap bigger animals and do it in a legal manner, I will teach them how to build more challenging traps, such as snares. I teach them to use the snares on squirrels so they can later cross over to larger animals. Snares are looped cords or rope that tighten when an animal walks through them. Generally, they are draped over some brush close to the ground. Sometimes sticks are placed in the ground to guide the animal into the snare. The snare is attached to a bent branch that snaps when the animal walks into the snare.

I also teach students to skin and dress the squirrel. A squirrel's anatomy is the same as a deer's, which is similar to ours except for the stomachs. When students and I trap a squirrel, I will demonstrate the cleaning and preparation process once very slowly. I expect them to be able to do it all the way through the next time.

I walk them through the anatomy, and I show in detail how to skin and clean the animal, showing them what to leave in and what to remove. You want to eat a certain amount of organs for the nutrients and fat content. The best for this are the heart, lungs, and kidneys. Others, like the gallbladder, stomach, and spleen, can be removed.

Because the animal has given his life for my benefit, I use all parts of the animal for something, except for the stomach. I discard the stomach because as bait it won't draw the type of animals I want to trap. Any leftover bits of flesh or meat after the cleaning process can be used for bait. Animal fat is ideal for cooking greens. Fat also supplements the lean meat to keep our digestive systems functioning properly. The bones can be filed into small tools, such as needles for sewing. The hides can be tanned and made into skins for a variety of uses. Even the skin of a squirrel can be made into a pouch.

To cook the squirrel meat, I lay it out flat and grill it. I try to carry rock salt to sprinkle on the meat.

In any hunt, I show my students how to read the health of the animal by looking at the fur. If the fur is dull or tattered, then they should probably leave the animal alone. Likewise if the animal is stumbling to the left then it probably has plague or is sick. Then when we catch the animal, I teach them how to look at the health of the liver and the glands. That will tell the overall health of the animal, and that also determines how much you should cook it. If the animal is extremely healthy, you could theoretically eat it raw. But if it has any signs of bad health or disease, then you want to make sure it is thoroughly cooked. In the worst case, if its liver is half gone, it has pussy glands, or it has worms in its meat, you might consider not eating it at all.

Students are less squeamish about the process than would seem to be the case. With small animals, they focus on what needs to be done. However, I find that with large animals, such as a deer we find dead by the roadside, students have trouble. The smell of skinning and preparing a deer is overpowering and weakens me even after all these years. The process itself is also physically taxing, as it takes over a day just to remove the skin.

Many people don't realize that we digest smell. It doesn't just go into our nose; it goes into our stomach and through our digestive system. When you have a bowel movement, that smell you have been inhaling comes out of you. Interestingly, this happens in cities as well—which should tell us something about how important our air is.

In our daily lives, we are often far removed from how much we destroy and kill animals and their environments. But we all do, maybe not with our own hands, but with our actions. As humans, we have to figure out what it takes to live, but also how to create balance and harmony in our environment to ensure long-term survival for all species. All of this makes hunting a major topic of discussion on the survival courses I teach.

Many of the people who come out on courses do so because they are looking for a gentler way of living with the earth. Some of these—I'd say about one in ten—extend that gentleness to veganism. Everybody on the course is respectful of one another's position. But what is interesting is that almost without exception, the vegans usually end up becoming re-solved during the course to the fact that it is better for them to eat meat, both for their health and for the ecological balance of the land.

I've illustrated this to students in many different areas and climates. When we enter an area, we can easily identify greens, roots, and berries that will make it possible for all of us to get enough nutrition and live healthfully for a couple months. But those are the prized foods for all mammals in the area, because they contain starches and sugars that sustain living things.

Once a student and I debated what respect for animals meant. He was a vegetarian, which is a very respectful way to live. He was on a course with me, living off the land in one very remote spot for ten days. The three-mile canyon was very rich in berries, which he would collect and eat each day. There was a huge squirrel population feeding off the same bushes. After a few days, I noticed that the berries were nearly depleted. I explained to him that we were starving the community of squirrels because we were not taking a balanced approach to the land. My reasoning was that it was better if we trapped a few squirrels, and then they would have less competition for the berries, thus creating a more balanced ecosystem. This is part of striking a natural balance in the environment to ensure survival for all.

Every environment is different. But the fact is that if a person finds the magic berry bush, there might be only one magic berry bush in a few-miles radius. A lot of animals are relying on that berry bush. If you just say, "I'm a vegan so I'm only going to eat berries," then you have just messed with a lot of animals.

The bottom line is that we should always strive to find the balance to live within a particular region. This is incumbent upon us, because as humans we have the intellect to look at the land and say: "There are only x number of wild onions, x number of berries, x number of cattails. I have to take into account a certain balance that will help everything out here. That means I will have to kill some animals, which will also help the cycle of all the animals competing for that bush."

That is how nature's balance is not only maintained but also improved.

Many vegans on courses examine the balance of the land and decide its natural order makes sense. While they end up eating an animal, both for the nutrition and the need to keep the land in balance, they almost always do not know what they will do when they return home. They are then forced to take that experience back home and figure out what to do with it. Some return to veganism, while others do start eating meat. They realize their body felt better, or they feel like they can buy free-range meat and create a better harmony that way. But no vegan goes home and starts eating hamburgers.

This becomes a topic of discussion. A mammal is very much like our flesh and blood. It has a family, raises its young, and acts a little bit like us instinctively. Killing something similar to us is difficult. Inevitably, the discussion turns to where the line is. Chickens are okay, and so are pigs—unless the person had a pet pig as a child. Dogs are not.

But when my students see hunting in the wild firsthand the talk always returns to the same place. It shows how far removed we are from our food supply. Most everyone has seen cattle grazing in a pasture, but few people think of that when they buy a Saran-wrapped tenderloin at the supermarket. The fact is, it is very hard to see the true cost of our food unless we watch it being separated from its environment.

Hunter-gatherers see this up close. It is very simple. They look at the land. They see what nature is telling them, and they look for a balance to make it better while still surviving.

Every time a hunter-gatherer walks into an area, he must have an awareness of the food supply. He must find the ability to live off the land. If he doesn't, he will die. Having the ability to live off the land makes you a seer.

Probably the deepest I delved into these issues with a student was on my journey with Jesse Perry from Flagstaff to Boulder. Jesse had a visceral reaction to hunting animals and preparing them to eat. When I killed the first rabbit for food, Jesse broke down in tears. Later, when I wanted to remove bird eggs from a nest, he adamantly refused to help. But what he saw caused him to question how we live in modern society.

After our journey, Jesse wrote a diary. He talked about being disgusted with the hypocrisies in himself that surfaced, the same hypocrisies that even the most caring consumer encounters every day. He crystallized the issue by writing that he wondered why he had trouble taking eggs from a bird's nest when he was famished in the wild, yet he had no problem eating an omelet at Denny's.

The fact is, we are so far removed from these issues in our culture that we must question ourselves at some point. Farm-to-table is a large movement, as is the humane treatment of animals we eat—all of which go through slaughterhouses. We want prime-grade, humanely raised animals. So we wrestle with this dilemma. We write books about these questions. We try to figure it out. But we ultimately cannot figure it out fully for the simple fact that most people are too far removed from the land.

Chapter Nineteen

TEACHING "THRIVAL"

The life-or-death element of being a true survivalist is not the daring. It's not being dropped by a helicopter into a jungle and trying to find your way out, like a TV show. It's not about the risk of doing something extreme like climbing the face of an icy glacier. It is more about the unknown, like walking through a vast desert without a map or compass and without knowing where your next water source is. Most consider that risk, but I consider it trust.

That separates me from other teachers. There is no trust from many teachers. For them, it's all about numbers. A lot of teachers must have a calculated formula that they can apply some kind of mathematical equation to. They need to know in terms of what the typical body goes through to get from point A to point B: "Am I going to compromise my health by not eating for a day?" They want it to be a scientific formula. And if the conclusion of science is that it is going to somehow be harmful, they won't do it.

I regard myself as a scientist, too. Science doesn't have all the answers, and neither do I. I'm seeking to find out if the facts are true. The point is that when someone thinks he is the final word on something, that's when you get yourself in trouble. This applies even more so in nature.

For most of human evolution, survival has been a way of life. Hunter-gatherers grew up learning nothing but survival. They had no choice. Nature is constantly changing and adapting. The tides may recede only to rise again, but no two tides rise alike. Survival skills must be applied in a fluid way that dovetails with the part of the earth you are on, and you must learn that area's rhythm, timing, and changes to be able to live there.

One truism I have learned from teaching survival courses and living in countless survival situations is that survival manuals offer only a vague outline of the necessary skills needed to live in the wilderness. Even worse, they can often give people a false sense of security that they have the means and tools to live off the land when, in fact, they do not. Survival is not a certificate you can pick up at a conference.

The fact of the matter is that if someone is relying solely on a survival manual, I guarantee they will not be able to live off the land for very long. A survival manual will force them to build things they don't need. Living off the land requires an intellect and understanding to ask questions. Where should a shelter go? What time of day should it be built? What time of day should a root be dug, or should that root even be dug up? Should an animal be collected in this spot because they are plentiful, or is there a reason why it should be collected somewhere else?

In short, the critical question is, where and how should a person invest their energy? In snow and cold, how and where someone invests their energy and the type of relationship they establish with the land will determine their success and maybe even their fate.

The lesson I underscore over and over is that there is no one answer for a survival scenario. I am the last person to give an answer. I want to know every single detail because I know there are a million different ways to answer the question.

One of the differences between what is understood about survival and the reality of survival is that many people believe that they have to use their energy while they have it. Survival books often teach that right from the get-go, the moment you are out the door, you must build tools quickly because you are going to start losing energy. But the land will resist that thinking.

When someone goes out full bore, he or she ends up making the wrong decisions. They haven't established any connection with the land. Consequently, they build things hastily, and those things don't work for them. The land wants to see somebody sit for a moment, contemplate, and ask themselves, "What should I do?" That's the space that many people don't utilize. A lot of people might think that is the lazy or the passive approach but it's really not.

Sometimes a student will see me running around at ninja-pace speeds. That is also a part of timing and rhythm. However, I have already built a deeper land connection so even if I am moving at a fast pace, I may actually be seeing more than the student moving slowly. Rhythm on the land is like a river that sometimes flows calmly and other times has rapids.

I teach my students that when they find themselves in a new environment, the best thing they can do is take a slow walk around and just observe everything. I tell them, don't try to collect anything or be productive. If there is a spot where it feels like they need to spend some time, I tell them to sit down or lie down, whatever their body feels like doing, and be open and receptive. Listen to the wind, the birds, and the animals. Then look around. Perhaps they will notice a nest in the distance, maybe berries over in nearby brush. But what I do know is that they will actually start seeing things that they wouldn't have seen if they charged out like a bull. This is a beginning level message, but it is critical.

On a more advanced level, there have been times that I have lain down and not fallen asleep. I have gone into a lucid stage and actually seen things about the surrounding area and had visions of them without having physically been to that place yet.

Most people go through life at one pace. In the wild, I have found that it is best to take in nature's immersions painfully slow and then at warp speed. After moving at the extremes, I then try to fill in the middle once I understand nature's timing. I think of nature as a song. The most beautiful note never feels old, even if another note does or does not follow it.

I tell students that if they reach that deeper level, if they sit down and start looking around and noticing more on either a physical or sub-conscious level, they will start absorbing the things around them. This will relax them and allow them to ask, "Based on my knowledge, what can I do with this to make this journey easier, more respectable, and more comfortable?" Not only will that cause them to make clearer de-cisions, it also will give them strength because they will have received energy from the land.

I emphasize that another important aspect is to take different paths. Instructors regularly fall into the rut of traveling the same path, rather than experimenting with a new one. For example, if the first time some-one collects water and follows the main trail because it was easier, then the next time they should take a brushy path back, and start investigat-ing the land to see what they can come to discover. Many, many times I have found food because I deviated from the main trail.

This thinking can tie into anyone's everyday life. If a person stays on the same path with their head pointed down, they are not going to be exposed to new opportunities. When you walk somewhere, try a differ-ent route. If you happen to be moving to a new place, go out, sit down, take a look around, and feel it. Maybe if you do that, you might find the place is not for you. The basic lesson is that you want to receive information. In nature, that is heightened and you can end up in a survival situation if you don't have that awareness.

Many people I've encountered know what works in their everyday lives, but somehow, they think that when they get out in nature, they have to change the rules. But they don't. If they start taking charge of things in their work life or in any situation when nobody knows who they are, they aren't going to get any respect. It's the same thing in nature; it will push you out. Even though those are two different worlds, the principle is very much the same. There is a clear overlap. People can act in nature the same way they do in a community. The difference is that if they try to impose themselves too much in the wilderness, they might annoy an African lion.

I can't lay down a formula for survival in a day or even a week because that would be called a survival handbook. Even if I did, the manual would be virtually useless. When I spend a couple weeks (or more) with students, they learn the patterns of nature that teach them how to look, where to look, and how to identify the characteristics of survival.

How do you not use excess energy? How do you receive energy without food? How do you make a shelter and a bed? How do you enjoy your experience in your shelter and your bed? How do you identify an edible plant? How does it feel? How does it smell? How does it taste? And most important, how do you knock out the word *survival* and turn it into a living situation?

By addressing these questions myself, I have become a better teacher. Students come out legitimately feeling comfortable they can survive, that it was a rewarding experience, and that they would do it again. They feel like they can even jump right back into it the next day if they had the time. The biggest lesson I have passed down to students is how to legitimately live off the land if they so desire. I've accomplished that by teaching them how to learn the natural flow and how to think for themselves.

Some people who enter my classes are thinking, *I have to learn how to survive.* But the word *survive* brings fear to people. That is a kind of fearmongering that comes from the exploitative TV survival shows. But I disabuse my students of that notion. I tell them that what I teach is the land. My ideal candidate is someone who wants to learn the land. I teach people how to live with the land in a fluid way that doesn't feel like a survival situation.

They watch as I apply the surroundings to our needs. I help them break things down to see what we need and what we don't. This makes it easier to navigate through complicated situations, such as tough terrain or a difficulty finding food. Interestingly, I've found that when people return to their normal lives, they use this to eliminate their baggage, to employ a pop psychology phrase. Baggage comes from holding on to things that made you comfortable when you were younger. However, these security boxes can end up blocking you from growth experiences, even though at one point they provided security.

Everybody has a different reaction to the wild. When city slickers set that first foot on the trail, they feel like they are in an alien environment. They walk for a while, get a few miles in, collect a few plants, and start to sense something magical unfolding. They become more focused and less distracted, as their daily worries fade into the landscape. On day two, they begin learning what it takes to live in the wild. Generally around day three, they wake up and feel like they have been hit upside the head because their diets are so different that detox kicks in. It is at that point that they realize there's no Chinese takeout available in the wilderness and the cuisine will be exotic plants and whatever we can hunt down together.

Even very healthy people feel like their strength level is cut in half. Everyone deals with this differently. Some feel like they are dying and moving only out of reflex; others wonder what it means. Jesse Perry likened the feeling to "an altered reality reminiscent of past experiences with psilocybin mushrooms," which, come to think of it, might be an inadvertent sales pitch to some prospects.

The positive people soon start to experience heightened sensations. All the rhythms in their body slow down, and they start seeing a lot more detail. For instance, they will see a bumblebee flying. It's no longer just a bee. They see every stripe and the fuzz on its abdomen. They see how its wings are moving to the point that they might even count the flaps per minute. They study the tips of its feet. This is the beginning of understanding their relationship with nature.

One thing I consider myself effective at is foreseeing problems that students may have. I pay such close attention to my students that it almost gives me headaches. I look at everyone individually and assess their skill level. I read over their medical histories to determine where the dangers may lie, see what medications they take, and find out specifics, such as if they have ever had an allergic reaction to a bee sting. Going into anaphylactic shock when you can rush to the emergency room is trying; going into anaphylactic shock in the wilderness is deadly.

Based on what I learn about each group of students, I am mindful of the footing and pacing. Many instructors push their students to the edge, to the point where they are going to tweak something, break an ankle, or have a bad fall.

The potential to foresee accidents is critical. Because students are off their normal diets and their blood sugar levels are reduced, extra care is required. I believe that everybody in America is partially diabetic, and it shows when they go out on a survival course. I haven't had anybody reach the point where they pass out for minutes at a time from low blood sugar, though many people have become dizzy and seen stars.

An instructor can't prevent accidents simply by safe protocol alone. In fact, the rules are less important than being able to properly assess all students' skill levels and coordinate that based on the environment.

I try to stay one step ahead and keep my students in balance. Once they dip too far, there is nothing in the wild that I can pick off a tree and immediately give them for an energy boost. There is no Snickers bar solution. When we first go out, I have students eat continuously to maintain their blood sugar.

I have had some students who are over seventy, so inevitably there are going to be some issues. The only serious problem I had occurred when I was guiding llama pack trips. A lady sat down on a log to tie her shoe and her artificial hip popped out of place. She was in excruciating pain.

I was a trained WFR, or wilderness first responder, meaning at that time I was certified to put a hip back into place. A WFR is a step up from being an EMT, but it's not as trained as a Wilderness EMT. As a woofer, I had learned to put shoulders, hips, and joints back into place, dress wounds, and give shots of adrenaline. We had also learned interesting techniques about sucking open chest wounds and how to build valves in the event of a chest puncture.

Hard as I tried, I could not get her hip joint back into place. I gave her Advil for the pain. She was a real trooper, but we needed medical help. Unfortunately, the company I worked for did not believe in guides carrying cell phones. We had no form of communication, and we were eight miles from the nearest trailhead. I took off sprinting and ran the eight miles in forty minutes to find a phone to call for a medevac.

The helicopter arrived twenty minutes later. The paramedics couldn't get her hip back into place, either, so they gave her relaxants and took her to the hospital. Fortunately, she made a full recovery.

The most practical aspect of survival in the wild is making a fire. I learned the process by reading a Tom Brown manual that contained poetic information about that magical tool. I took that manual, along with fifteen others books, to the Sierras and studied the skills, for myself and so I could teach students.

At first, I struggled mightily, rubbing two sticks together for hours and ending up with nothing but blisters. But over time I became very proficient and learned that there are many natural ways to bring dead wood to life. One thing I learned from Tom Brown's teachings in his books and from my students who have taken his classes (as I have not met him) is that he often leaves out important information to push students to gain more out of the process. I liken it to the way a Shaolin monk makes his pupil sweep a floor for two years before teaching him a basic karate kick.

Brown favored what is known as coyote teaching. The term comes from Native American lore. Many Native Americans believe that animals contain different aspects of our personalities. Coyotes are considered to be slightly mischievous with traits of a child. The coyote still needs to grow up, but at the same time, it has that childlike ability to draw people in.

Brown had a different way of doing things. I always had an innate ability to figure out things for myself. I looked at books as very rough guidelines. For me, it was still about looking at all the pieces and trying to figure out the solution. But as a teacher, I prefer a more direct approach.

The only coyote teaching I will do is to figure out a way to trick somebody to sit in a particular spot for a long period of time. Or if I realize that someone has citified personality traits, I might use those in a coyote way to spark their interest in the natural world.

As a teacher, I pride myself on giving very clear and fully detailed lessons so the students understand the information without being frustrated. What I have learned is that as a species we are so incompetent in the wild that if I started trying to trick people and make it harder, they would give up. It is critical for me to maintain their passion so that they feel successful. I prefer looking at methods that are rooted in ancient ways because they are just as good in the present day as they were a thousand years ago.

There are many secrets to making fire without any man-made aids. The main thing I teach my students to focus on are the properties of the wood. If you are creating a primitive fire, most are variations on what is called friction fire. This involves figuring out a way to create friction between two pieces of wood. The main issue is that the grains of wood must be short. They cannot be long and splintery; otherwise they will not create a coal that is fine and dark. A fine, dark coal holds together.

All friction woods have an infinite amount of combinations that work for different reasons. If the wood is too hard, then I find that I have to apply too much muscle to create the bond or friction. However, if a root is too soft, then one piece of wood drills through the other. To check for hardness, I push my thumb into the root. If it dents easily, the wood is too soft.

The wood should be bone dry, meaning it's dead, though in nature there are always exceptions to the rule. For example, sagebrush almost works better when it's completely alive. There are short pores through the structure that create the right type of char. Sagebrush works well for a bow drill (where you wrap the drill stick in the strands of a bow) but can be very difficult with a hand drill (where you rub your palms on the drill stick). In snow or heavy rain, I look for places where trees have grown over and created pockets where I can dig and find dry material. Sometimes I have to carve into the wood several inches to find out if the wood is dry enough.

The bow drill has a mechanical advantage. But without any technology, it requires more work to build. In North America, the hand drill was used almost exclusively by all Native American tribes. The way the user kneels and places his hands together resembles someone praying. With the proper knowledge, skill, and wood, it is extremely efficient—like a big, primitive lighter.

The environment often dictates what I can do. If I am in a snowy area at a higher elevation, it is unlikely that I will find usable firewood. Knowing this in advance, I will collect wood at a lower elevation before climbing. If I am in a pure survival situation, I will hike down or wait for it to stop snowing. The word for that is *patience*. I build a shelter, hunker down, and go hungry for a couple days. The advantage of fasting and staying put is that I slow down my metabolism. I don't fight the land. I let it teach me and then when it opens back up, I find my rhythm.

Safety is paramount. I always clear a large ten-to-fifteen-foot-diameter circle of all the debris, grass, leaves, and everything around that area. I kick it out with my feet so I am left with only soil, dirt, or sand. Then I build a fire pit in the very center of that area. More important than building a solid ring is clearing the area.

The reason most forest fires start is that people don't remove surrounding grass and debris. They come upon a place where there is dead grass, put some rocks down for a border, and build a small ring for the fire. Problem is, the fire is almost always going to jump the ring and catch the grass.

Another issue I have seen is roots. If someone digs a fire pit and hits a dead root and builds a fire on it, there is a chance that root will smolder back into the tree. If the ground is not damp and there is even the smallest bit of an air pocket allowing oxygen to travel along that burning root, it will reach the tree and the tree will catch fire.

The following morning, I teach students how to deal with the remains of fires. Some people just leave them. I insist my students go overboard to instill a certain order of respect with the fire. I have them take the leftover coals and grind them up into a powder. I then have them mix the ground coals with leftover dung from whatever animal is around and spread that mixture into the brush so it creates a fertile soil and provides nitrogen to the plants. This leaves the areas better off than when we arrived.

Sometimes when I'm trying to avoid any impact at all and I just want to stop and cook up a lunch meal, I will find an island in the river or build a fire right on the edge of the water line, where it is free of all debris. When the fire is done, I will scoop the ashes back into the water, knowing that area will eventually get flooded over. The ashes don't harm the water because it disperses the coals over miles and miles. The island is also a safe place for inexperienced people to build a fire, because the fire is unlikely to jump the water and start a forest fire.

In my mind, human roots lie deeper in fire than in any other force of nature. If we go way back in time to when man first harnessed fire, most likely they saw lightning strike. They probably kept their fires going by adding sticks for kindling. They sat around those fires in the cold and were warmed. The fire sculpted the people. Instead of using their furs to keep them warm, they hung out around the fire, and it created community time.

Fire also moved us away from being animals, as most animals run from fire. That was a huge shift. Archaeologists always say what separates man from animal is his ability to use tools, but we're now finding out that animals can use tools, such as a monkey using a stick to plunge into an ant hole and pull out the ants. But likely it was fire that separated man from animal, as undomesticated animals do not sit around a fire.

The common word used in the survival community for converting a survival situation into a living situation is *thrival*.

Thrival is a state that occurs when the layer of desperation and the feeling of fighting to live (or be rescued, if that's the case) is replaced by the joys of nature. At that point, a person achieves a feeling of place and belonging. It is a place where nature is no longer their enemy numbering their days on the planet. In thrival, they become a big part of nature and would be able to live there indefinitely, if they so chose, because they have succumbed to nature's turns and are beginning to thrive, instead of just survive.

There are two primary aspects to thrival: starting the journey being open to possibilities, and being able to stay with the journey knowing you will never completely arrive at a destination or conquer it. The process of thrival begins simply enough, by adopting a positive attitude and by truly enjoying the place you are in. The beautiful thing about being open is that the earth will reveal its secrets, and your passion for the journey will grow with each one. But know that no one will ever find them all.

In a state of thrival in nature, a person achieves a feeling of pure bliss, which is the second primary aspect. At that point, they are no longer an alien on the planet. They are not separated from the earth by technology and modern gadgetry, but are rather in a place where the earth becomes their family and they find an indelible connection to it. We all need this in varying degrees, regardless of where we are.

This entry into thrival can be extended to any place or situation you find yourself in, not just in nature. It could be a new town, new job, or new house. Whatever the journey, being able to stay with it for a long period of time takes training, knowledge, and patience.

As a teacher, I've had the opportunity to work with hundreds, if not thousands, of students from all walks of modern and submodern life. I have watched them relate to the land, seen what sticks with them, and what they take away from the experience and apply to their everyday lives. From what I have seen, people on social levels and people in nature are very similar, but in a mental capacity, things are much different. We are striving too hard for technology and have become trapped in the dogma of scientific thinking. This has pulled us away from the land. There is also evidence, cited frequently by Paul Shepard and others, that shows that our brain capacity is shrinking now that we have moved away from the hunter-gatherer lifestyle.

There are different types of intelligence and smarts—social, business, mathematical, and hunter-gatherer. Each type of smarts functions well in a specific place. What I have learned is that in society everything is very linear. Society demands a routine where things consistently function the same. But in nature, that is not possible. Everything is constantly growing and changing in infinite shapes. Not one limb is the same in nature, but at a hardware store, every piece of lumber is the same. In our society, we have created a formula for putting everything into its slot. In nature, that cannot be done, and that is threatening to people. It takes a certain intellect to work with something that is not straight. I think we have lost that capacity.

Take a rocket scientist dropped into nature—literally. I actually had one as a student on a survival course. I gave him an intermediate task: setting a trap with natural materials. Nothing in nature grows straight so you must have the mental flexibility to piece together things in a natural way that allows the trap to stay in place and spring at the right moment. Teaching the rocket scientist to set that trap became a great test of my patience. It made me realize that someone who is a genius can be completely inept at understanding the natural world.

Students will often come to a course with the reference point that hunter-gatherers are our "primitive" past. But I teach them that from my experience of living in the wilderness for more than two decades, I can say with near certainty that those habitants of our primitive past had a greater mental capacity than we realize, or can even comprehend. Here's my point to them: someone cannot dominate the wilds because he or she has a strong modern intellect. In fact, to be a thrivalist they must adopt a completely different set of rules.

The first two virtues I impress upon students are patience and not alienating yourself. Being patient means the ability to stay open to possibilities and look and listen to what the land needs and what the person needs in return. That is often the reason Native Americans practiced vision quest circles. Sitting in a five-to-nine-foot circle of stone for four days and four nights without food and water makes you patient.

Not alienating oneself in nature means that a person often needs to leave technology—in the form of common, purchased survival tools—out of the wilderness experience. This may mean leaving behind a favorite knife and relying on rocks and other natural sharp edges in nature for cutting. By doing this, yes, survival is technically harder. However, what I tell my students they will find is that they will want to stay with the experience longer because they are doing it on their terms.

Everybody is born with different thought processes and patterns.

Some people are very good at concentration and laserlike focus, whereas others have more dispersed focus. Today, we label that as ADD and ADHD. Interestingly, people with ADD and ADHD actually excel in the wilderness because you need dispersed focus to be able to talk to somebody while hearing the sounds of nature at the same time. The ability to have your focus bounce around can be very helpful. There are many things happening at once in the wild. Focusing too closely on just one thing can cause you to miss something important.

If you think your job is complex—whether you are an electrical engineer, a tax lawyer, or a television executive—spending time in nature may be a stark and ultimately beautiful awakening to true complexity. It may help you simplify and streamline your everyday life. We often think of nature as simple, but it's quite the opposite. I have had students who were doctors, lawyers, hippies, jocks, naturalists, comedians, musicians, and belly dancers, and regardless of their professions and backgrounds, they have all benefited from being in nature.

Being an instructor, I have learned that I can take something I love more than myself, my passion for the land, and share it with others, and see how they respond. The best way to learn, I have concluded, is to teach.

People who return from the wilderness are never the same. Though at home they return to comfort foods, most of them eat far less highly processed foods and more natural foods. Their anxieties are softened, and they are easier to be around. Many tell me that they achieve a better balance in their lives. I find that when they do small tasks that help the environment, such as recycling, they feel that they know what they are saving.

Learning to survive in the wild even for short periods can translate to handling fear in the everyday world. Whenever I'm scared—say in a TV audition, which can be scarier than many places in the wild—I step back and ask myself what the bigger picture is. If I can see it, then I can isolate that one spot, and move forward without being consumed by feelings of fear. I believe the same is true in much scarier situations. If you can see that bigger picture—even if it is not the ultimate bigger picture of your life continuing—you can condition yourself to relax and push forward.

What I find from my students who establish a connection with the land is that they realize the potential of what they can be as a human being on a physical and even spiritual level, and it makes them want to return for more. After we are out for a month, they will develop themselves in ways they have never experienced. Sometimes they push themselves so hard that they feel enlightenment, but at the same time, they are craving a cheeseburger and an ice cream sandwich. They return to their city lives and get all those things they were dreaming about on the trail, but when they lose that wilderness boost and that feeling of peace and sanity, they almost always return for more.

There used to be a point where I thought people could find peace and sanity without nature. But from my students, I found that people who find peace and sanity do so because they are usually taking a moment to acknowledge a little bit of nature around them.

EPIC SURVIVAL LESSON:
PUT YOUR FEET IN THE DIRT

What I want most of all is for people to have a burning need to understand the ground we live on, and be willing to set aside their preconceived notions to learn from the smallest and grandest of all things. I want to inspire people to be closer to the earth in its rawest form. I am now convinced that the only way to access the human spirit is through creating your own intimate relationship with the land.

To me, it is about learning the wisdom of the wilderness at a time when far too many view it, at worst, as material to be plowed down if it gets in the way of urban development, or at best, something to gawk at through a car window or in a coffee table book. Most people have in some way felt a special connection to the wilderness at one time or another. This connection goes beyond the recesses of the mind. It's something that cries out: "Wake up! The landscape is right in front of you. It is real, and it is where your spirit can thrive."

It boils down to not isolating ourselves too much from nature. The more ways we can find to put our feet in the proverbial dirt, the better we will be in all aspects of our lives.

Chapter Twenty

A BAREFOOT
WILDERNESS RUN

The sun had not yet come up. I walked outside wearing shorts and a light shirt to go for a run. I didn't need shoes for this run. I was in a place where I had never been, and I wanted to connect with this new land. My legs have always taken me to the places I needed to go. Today, I hoped they would carry me somewhere special.

I started slowly. I didn't know the area. It felt slightly foreign, but as with all places I have been around the world, it was also somewhat familiar. The ground was rough but forgiving. The more comfortable I felt, the more I lengthened my stride. Soon, I forgot I was running. The ground was simply moving under me—the zazen of running—which allowed me to take notice of my surroundings.

The first thing I noticed was a large tree that forked in four directions. It seemed to be pointing to the right toward a trail, so I took it.

The trail narrowed. On the right, there was a massive area of ancient bedrock protruding from the ground. As I passed, I saw mica flecks and lines in the stone that had been shaped millions of years ago. I wondered how many different bands of tribes had walked over the rock. Nearby, on a sweet birch tree branch, two squirrels wrestled for space.

I pressed on to see what the immediate future held. The trail dipped down and then popped up. Eventually I passed a pond. With each step,

I felt small pebbles nudging between my toes. They weren't sharp but rather round and worn, oddly soft in way, likely from being walked on for generations.

The sun was mounting the sky. I spotted a smaller path and exited the trail to explore it. A near-perfect canopy of trees was overhead. I stayed close to the water. Water always leads to more life. I felt alone, but I wasn't.

From all sides, people were emerging from connecting trails. They were very much like me; they were out enjoying the natural world.

Following the water, I hooked to the left. The sun had crested the horizon, and it hit me squarely in the eyes. I was heading east. I ran another mile or so, and continued to hug the water. It moved me to the south, and the sun was no longer in my eyes.

I could hear more people joining me. I didn't look back, but they were there. They weren't chasing me, or threatening to pass. Even though I knew they were on their own, it felt like they were joining me.

With the sun fully hidden by trees, I looked up. I saw in front of me, not more than a half mile away, one of the most beautiful structures I had ever laid eyes on. It was yellow stone, so perfectly shaped that I slowed down for a better look. I held my breath at its beauty. I kept looking up, up, up. It was as tall as a mountain.

The structure was two massive rock towers rising from a common point with a plateau in the center. In the sunlight, the towers glowed. It was nothing like the rock formations in the western United States, as it was perfectly sculpted.

Marveling, I continued my run. I passed a line of oak cattails. On the other side, I heard dogs barking, but I couldn't see them.

I looked up again. In front of me was a row of shiny structures. Everything looked like pure glass, and each one reflected off the other. Just behind them, one towered above the rest. The structure rose straight up so high only man could have conceived it.

I stopped and moved off the trail. I looked around. Hundreds of people were there, running and walking. People were walking their dogs. Just past two guys tossing a Frisbee was a metal cart with a picture of a hot dog on top. I watched a few joggers pass. None of them looked down at my bare feet.

It was my first run in Central Park, and my first morning ever being in New York City.

Millions of people were waking up around me and going off to make their futures. But these few hundred in Central Park realized that the natural world was right in front of them. Central Park is the one piece of land in New York City that has been comparably less disrupted than the rest of the city.

The people in the park seemed to fall into two categories. Some were going places, with purpose. Others were simply enjoying their steps. They were breathing the air, taking in the beauty of nature, and perhaps wondering how a row of hundred-year-old magnolias could form such a perfect canopy. The consensus, however, seemed to be that if you can survive outside the park, you can survive in it.

When you realize what the wild can do for you, there is a desire to mesh it with the modern world, even if you are not going to quit your job and become a hunter-gatherer. We know what nature can do for people who live in urban environments. We know it can build their awareness, their physicality, and their senses, and all of these can be adapted into their everyday lives. In our society today, the earth underneath us has become a distant thing. For the most part, we live in a concrete world removed from the true ground. These people could easily trap themselves in a concrete existence, but chose to step off the concrete and onto the land.

I stood there, staring up at the most beautiful buildings I had ever seen. They were designed and built with architectural integrity. But in my mind, no man's artistic creation, no feat of architecture, will ever compare to the beauty of the earth.

As I looked around, I wondered, *How do I fit with these people? I live near a town of a couple hundred people. The people around me now live in a city of eight million. We have completely different baselines.*

My hunter-gatherer lifestyle has led me to struggle in this reality on occasion. Relationships with women, for one, have been a challenge. In a bar, I sometimes have trouble communicating in modern-speak with members of the opposite sex. Not long ago, a stunning young lady came up to me and told me I was strikingly handsome. I'm not sure what I said, but it wasn't the right thing because she smiled and walked away.

Even when a woman understands my lifestyle, there can be complications. Once a girlfriend was living with me in my primitive dwelling in Utah and a mountain lion that fascinated me would visit every night. She became freaked out, so I scared off the mountain lion. We soon broke up, but I never saw the mountain lion again.

The rules of everyday life can often be foreign to me in comical ways. For example, when I was in Los Angeles last year I checked into a nice hotel. I was pleasantly surprised to find a refrigerator stocked with snacks and drinks. I was even more surprised to find that after I consumed many of the items, the hotel restocked them like my mother refilling the fridge. Problem was, when I checked out I got hit with a $551 minibar bill. I had no idea the snacks weren't complimentary.

As I travel to different cities, there is not the same type of weight on me as I see on many other people. Being in survival situations has taught me what it takes to live. That connection is very powerful. It has developed all my senses. I have experienced heightened hearing, clearer eyesight, and cleaner smell. My sixth sense comes alive, and it makes me realize the potential of what I can be as a human being. All of that breeds contentment.

Still, I often look up at the sky and ask the creator where I fit into all of this. How wild am I supposed to be? How human? How much are these supposed to be intertwined? I always come to the same conclusion: it is going to take a lifetime to find the answers.

But what pushes me forward, what inspires me, is seeing people who want to connect to the earth in any way, as these people in Central Park were doing. I believe it's important not to wait for tomorrow, but to start today. If someone has an interest in nature, they should start by going out and getting in it. If that takes ten minutes out of the day, take the ten minutes. It can't be a matter of "I'll wait for the weekend." A weekend is an awesome time to get outside, but making it a daily practice is better. In our culture today, for most people, if they don't do something on a daily basis, it will slip out of their routine, which is just human nature.

For me, tapping into the natural laws of one environment is very applicable when you travel to a different environment, no matter how dissimilar to yours. I have lived off the land in a jungle of Kauai, in the California desert, in the Sierra mountains. I have explored the plains of Tanzania, the rain forests of Costa Rica, and the jungles of Vietnam, and now I had run in Central Park. What I have learned from traveling to all these places is that the earth is vast, but it's not such a big place.

Even though my reference point with the land was vastly different from that of everyone in Central Park that morning, I felt as if I was sharing my connection to a new place with the people who knew it well. It didn't matter that they weren't on a walkabout in Arizona, or on a mesa in the Kaiparowits, or at ten thousand feet on the Pacific Crest Trail. They were enjoying the wilderness that was right in front of them. And I felt that if I kept running through the trails of Central Park, some new secrets of the earth might reveal themselves to me.

ACKNOWLEDGMENTS

Matt would like to thank:

My good friend Dave Nessia, who has been a great coteacher, walk-about partner, and a mentor of the human spirit, and my good friend Breck Crystal, who has been my equal and more in so many aspects throughout our primitive-skills journey.

David Holladay, who shared his vast plant and primitive-skills wisdom of the Boulder, Utah, area.

Kirsten Rechnitz, who was my partner and a gifted woman who shared time with me living in a pit house and a wigwam, as well as on the trail.

The Native American people for showing me their earth wisdom and ancient roots.

Vikki Thorn, Hannah Oohwiler, Matt Thorn, Eric Scott, and Raymond Shurtz for being a huge inspiration in bringing heart and life to the journeys of music and voice.

My dad for taking me on those long hikes in the mountains, and my mom for indulging me with so much ocean time.

My grandma and grandfather for teaching me spirit and integrity.

Dave Wescott, who has been one of the greatest bridges for bringing primitive skills to mainstream lives.

Jamie Grossman Young, my manager, who has helped make possible so many new opportunities for me in TV and publishing.

ACKNOWLEDGMENTS

Larry and Judy Davis for being like second parents when I moved to Boulder, Utah.

All my TV friends and coworkers, who have shared joys and hardships on our worldwide adventures to bring the world of survival to mainstream TV.

Friends and teachers at the Boulder Outdoor Survival School (BOSS) for our journeys and growth together.

Friends and family at the Winter Count gathering for being such a close tribe.

All my students, who have at times taught me more than I may have taught them.

The rock for teaching me how to "dance."

And the earth for teaching so much.

Matt and Josh would like to thank:

Andrew Stuart, our agent, for showing his enthusiasm for this project when it was an amorphous idea, guiding it through the proposal stage, and working his usual magic in finding us the best publisher.

Mitchell Ivers, who was our first choice to edit this book. He is the consummate writer's editor who knows how to bring out the best in any manuscript regardless of the subject matter. Not only are we thankful he stepped up and bought the book at the proposal stage, but we are even more grateful for his advice on constructing a narrative that delivered on all aspects of Matt's story.

The first-rate team at Gallery Books: Louise Burke (the boss who sets the professional tone), publisher Jen Bergstrom, director of publicity Jennifer Robinson, publicist Meagan Brown, art director Lisa Litwack, managing editor Susan Rella, senior production editor Jessica Chin, marketing director Liz Psaltis, and last but certainly not least, assistant editor Natasha Simons, who babysat the book at all stages, and Stephanie Evans Biggins for her sure-handed copyedit of the manuscript.

Jesse Perry, who wrote a wonderful diary that helped recall the events of his walk with Matt from Arizona to Utah.

Dr. Sam Parnia for his medical insights into what the body goes through in extreme conditions, and Ryan Koch for his thoughts on nutrition in the wild.

Bulletin of Primitive Technology (www.btprimitives.com) for granting permission to use Matt's original drawings that first appeared in the magazine.